A WILLING HEART

Selflessly serving others often sounds good in theory but can be near-impossible to put into practice in our day-to-day lives. Marci Alborghetti's wonderful new book challenges us to go outside our comfort zones to walk the road of love and service, and to do it with joy. Following in the footsteps of St. Francis of Assisi, she urges us to preach more through our actions than our words.

Mary DeTurris Poust
Author of *Walking Together*

In *A Willing Heart*, Marci Alborghetti offers an abundance of stories from scripture, saints, and her own life, as well as encouragement and suggestions for concrete ways to extend oneself in generous-hearted service to others. This inspiring book fills a specific gap and could not be more timely.

Christine Valters Paintner
Author of *Water, Wind, Earth, and Fire*

There's a prayer that ends with these words: "Give the world the best you have and you may be kicked in the teeth. Give the world your best anyway." Hard words. Marci Alborghetti has some sound advice for those of us stuck in one or more of these "reasons" not to be of service in the world. The advice is practical, accessible and transforming, grounded in the marvelous parables and sayings of Jesus, illuminated by references to the saints and to ordinary people reaching out to others with what they had. The author invites us to think about how much we have been given, how much we really need, and (for the sake of love and being fully alive) how much we need to give away, give back.

Alan Jones
Dean Emeritus
Grace Cathedral, San Francisco

Provocative, thoughtful, gentle challenging, urging responsibility—a conscience-raising read—it is all there . . . a manual to be a better human being.

Marylouise Fennell, R.S.M.
Senior Counsel
Council of Independent Colleges

This is a gem of a book! Marci presents both the joy and the challenge of service with great insight into the opportunities God presents to us and the way in which we can and do respond. Her examples from both the lives of the saints and her own grace-filled journey are very real and prompt me to say, "I could do that!" or "I have done that." or maybe, "Could I really do that?" The format at the end of each chapter with scripture, prayer, questions for consideration, and suggestions for service lends itself to individual and group reflection. Everyone reading *A Willing Heart* will feel both affirmed and encouraged by what service they currently give and invited to embrace service as a focus in all of their decision making.

Margaret Crowley, R.S.M.
Holy Cross Hospital, Fort Lauderdale

A WILLING HEART

HOW TO
serve
WHEN YOU THINK
YOU CAN'T

MARCI ALBORGHETTI

ave maria press AMP notre dame, indiana

© 2011 by Marci Alborghetti

Founded in 1865, Ave Maria Press is a ministry of the Indiana Province of Holy Cross.

www.avemariapress.com

ISBN-10 1-59471-248-4   ISBN-13 978-1-59471-248-7

Cover image © Olaf Kowalzik–Commercial Collection/Alamy

Cover and text design by Brian C. Conley.

Printed and bound in the United States of America.

Library of Congress Cataloging-in-Publication Data

Alborghetti, Marci.
  A willing heart / Marci Alborghetti.
    p. cm.
  Includes bibliographical references.
  ISBN-13: 978-1-59471-248-7 (pbk.)
  ISBN-10: 1-59471-248-4 (pbk.)
  1. Service (Theology) 2. Hospitality--Religious aspects--Christianity. 3. Home--Religious aspects--Christianity. I. Title.
  BT738.4.A43 2011
  248.4--dc22

                                    2010049943

green press
INITIATIVE

For GOD.
To Charlie,
and the Saint James Literary Club,
especially in memory of William Main.

Contents

Foreword

In today's challenging times, needs often seem to outweigh the available resources to address them. At the same time, we are reminded that the tangible power of human contact, a warm welcome, and a compassionate and listening heart are resources that know no bounds. In fidelity to the mission of Jesus, we call one another to offer hope and consolation, help and comfort to each other when hearts are heavy, when life is difficult, when needs seem insurmountable.

The ministry of Christian service is a palpable expression of such sacred hospitality. Through the ministry of serving, we invite one another to be at home, to come home, to be welcomed home in heart and soul and body. Home is that place where we hear the words, "We love you." Home is a place where we can go even when we have fallen flat on our faces—trusting that someone will be there to help pick us up. Home is a place where someone says to us, "I'm so happy you're here!" Home is a place where I belong, a place where I will never be shut out. Home is an expression of God's limitless care. Marci Alborghetti understands that real Christian service begins in the home, and her book, *A Willing Heart,* is a warm, commonsense vision of Christian service and how it can be done right at home.

Christian service is the act of welcoming one another home. Those who step out into the sacred ministry of service do so fully aware of their own limitations and human struggles, for such holy service issues from a generous, willing, and wise heart. They do so fully cognizant that welcoming one another home is an act grounded in faith, filled with compassion, and alive in the assurance that God will always be there with open arms.

Some time ago, I read a wonderful little book on, of all things, the martial arts. In the chapter entitled "A Glimpse of Wisdom," the author describes the wise person as one who embraces vulnerability, who expands the heart, sees humor, and throws one's arms around ambiguity.[1] The wise and compassionate person is capable of living the unobtrusive life of humility and is welcoming toward everyone. It strikes me that this is not a bad description of what those engaged in Christian service express in their profound and humble act of welcoming their sisters and brothers to find a warm and hospitable home in our community of faith.

The ministry of service, grounded in prayer and in the gospel, leads us into the very crevices of the soul where we make our home in God. It is there we discover that fragility and questioning are perhaps more honest and far truer than any illusions of power or certitude in believing we have all the right answers. The ministry of service in the name of Jesus beckons us to stand in wonder before one another as we stand in awe before the breath of God and are welcomed into the warmth of home in the communion of faith.

In our steady longing to find our home in God and to accompany our sisters and brothers there, our hearts expand beyond judgment, and we are led to that space of compassion and mercy.

In the pages that follow, you will take a very special path toward home. You will be invited into the heart of the gospel and into the holy spaces of the soul to garner the strength and the wisdom to minister humbly and well. May your heart and your soul find joy and consolation as you walk anew with wonderful companions toward that welcoming home in the community of faith and love.

Donna J. Markham, O.P.

Introduction

Not long ago in the city where I live, some city council members tried to shut down my church's emergency homeless shelter. They contended that the shelter was attracting an undesirable element to our downtown area, and they weren't enthusiastic about allowing a faith-based nonprofit organization to address what they felt was a city-government issue. But the council members had a problem. They couldn't close the shelter by cutting funds, since the city didn't pay for the service. Nor could they eject it from its physical home, since the shelter was the cramped basement of our church. The homeless men and women who slept at the shelter came in after 7:00 p.m. and were out by 7:00 a.m. each day; many were day laborers, veterans, and people suffering with physical or mental illnesses. At the shelter, they received a snack, a cot, and a chance to socialize and seek help.

In the end, the only thing the council could do to get rid of the shelter was officially to resolve to disallow it. This they did. In response, something of a melee ensued, with public hearings, committees, negotiations, and the kind of media coverage that made residents cringe. Meanwhile, some in the city's faith community talked of protests, civil disobedience, and even of immediately closing the shelter themselves, thus forcing the city, along with its police department and hospital, to deal with the consequences.

As a volunteer who'd come to know and care for many of the shelter guests and staff, I was deeply disturbed by what was turning into a circus. My husband, Charlie, had fought to get the shelter established and was suddenly fighting to save it. Increasingly, it seemed to us, the situation was unfolding with little or no consideration for the shelter residents themselves, who should have been everyone's central concern. The city council claimed it was serving and protecting the city. While some council members supported the shelter in theory, others felt that the specter of homelessness spoiled the city's image. There was already public housing, they argued; why must there be a shelter as well? Why risk offending visitors and downtown businesses?

On the other hand, the outraged members of the faith community claimed they were serving the city by forcing it to confront the consequences of a prospective closure. Closing this haven, they contended, would mean more work for the police, the hospital emergency room, and the city's poorly funded and under-staffed social services. It would put on the streets people who were victims of joblessness, war, illness, and broken relationships. Each side declared that it was serving the city. But who, I wondered, in the midst of this political (and ego) driven contest, was really serving the homeless?

And who was serving God?

The situation with our homeless shelter opened a floodgate of questions for me. What is Christian service, really? We Christians speak of our love for Jesus. Loving Jesus is easy; following Him is not. Do we really love Jesus if we ignore His frequent exhortations to service? And how do we open ourselves to the God-given grace that makes service possible?

Can we freely enjoy a bountiful church potluck supper if people are going hungry in our community, or for that matter, in the world? Can we revel in new winter coats or Easter clothes when someone shivers in rags on a street corner? Should we support policies—local, national, or global—that exclude and alienate the very people Jesus told us to feed, clothe, visit, and care for? And if we cannot support such policies, how do we not support them? With our votes? With public protests and civil disobedience? With trade embargoes? Are those things enough, or must we step in and do God's work where governments fail and falter?

These questions make us uncomfortable. They make *me* uncomfortable! I want to protest, "Wait! What am I supposed to do about all this? Don't I have a responsibility to take care of myself, my own? If I give away all my time and substance, who will take care of me and those depending upon me? Won't I then become part of the problem and not the solution?"

These are valid concerns. Service is not easy in our unstable economy and acquisitive culture. But as disturbed as they sometimes make me feel, the gospels leave no question about what Jesus asks of us. We are to love and serve the Father with a willing heart in everything we say, think, feel, and do. The most important questions the gospels provoke are: what is our answer to what Jesus asks of us? Are we willing to serve? Am I willing to do this?

The truth is, I come nowhere near to loving Him with my actions as deeply as I claim to love Him with my heart and mind. That's where God's grace comes in. No one can move forward in any ministry without first accessing grace. Just like God's presence, God's grace is there for the taking. Without it, we can do so little, only what our human nature allows. With grace, we rely on God to help us stretch beyond our sometimes narrow perspectives on what we can and cannot do. Grace loosens the limits we set upon ourselves.

I've discovered this firsthand—sometimes the hard way. The few faltering steps I've taken on the road to service have not been taken early or quickly or boldly enough. Yet these steps, and the people I've met along the way, have taught me a great deal. I hope, in the following pages, to share what I've learned. This book will show how we can better serve God and others by providing examples, practical suggestions, anecdotes, and inspiration. It will explore Jesus' message and the way in which all of scripture yearns toward service while emphasizing the fundamental role of grace in our lives and our decisions. I pray that through my rather ordinary journey and the sometimes extraordinary journeys of those I've been blessed to know, as well as saints and other towering models of service, we can come to serve Jesus as much as we love Him. We are all "unprofitable servants," but perhaps, seeking grace, step by step, we can become a little more profitable.

"Then the king will say to those on his right, 'Come, you that are blessed by my Father. Inherit the kingdom prepared for you from the foundation of the world; for I was hungry and you gave me food, I was thirsty and you gave me something to drink, I was a stranger and you welcomed me, I was naked and you gave me clothing, I was sick and you took care of me, I was in prison and you visited me.' Then the righteous will answer him, 'Lord, when was it that we saw you hungry and gave you food, or thirsty and gave you something to drink? And when was it that we saw you a stranger and welcomed you, or naked and gave you clothing? And when was it that we saw you sick or in prison and visited you? And the king will answer them, 'Truly I tell you, just as you did it to one of the least of these who are members of my family, you did it to me.'"

Matthew 25:34–41

CHAPTER ONE

Wake Up

"But I say to you . . . Love your enemies, do good to those who hate you, bless those who curse you, pray for those who abuse you. If anyone strikes you on the cheek, offer the other also; and from anyone who takes away your coat do not withhold even your shirt. Give to everyone who begs from you; and if anyone takes away your goods, do not ask for them again. Do to others as you would have them do to you."

LUKE 6:27–31

From the pulpit, the Jesuit priest asked a question that Christians have been muttering under their breath for more than two thousand years: "How am I supposed to love someone I don't even like?" Suddenly you could hear a pin drop in the church. No more restless rustling; no sneaking glances at wristwatches; no coughing, throat clearing, or whispered admonitions from parents to children; no suppressed giggling. Everyone wanted to hear the answer to this one.

As it turned out, the answer was simple, but not easy. We can't love people we dislike if we think of love as a feeling that floods through us unbidden, the priest said. We can't love the stranger or the aggravating person or the greedy distant relative, if we wait to be moved by the same glowing emotion we feel for someone we care deeply for or are in love with. We can't love the way Jesus asks us to love if we think of love as a passive emotion, something that happens to us. If we are to love those we don't like, we must think of love as an act of will, an action we take and not a feeling that overwhelms us—a verb and not a noun. We must accept God's invitation, indeed, God's example, and decide to love; then, as Nike has told us for years now, we need to "just do it."

You could almost hear the groans in that church. This was not the answer everyone had been waiting for. We were hoping for some magic words, some miracle-working trick that would transform us into people who could "love our neighbor as ourselves" with no effort at all, regardless of how much our neighbor annoyed us. Perhaps some of us were even hoping that the priest would let us off the hook completely, assuring us that "love your neighbor" was just a nice concept that Jesus couldn't possibly expect us to fully embrace. This idea of love as an act of will was not the antidote that we'd envisioned to a combative, difficult, stressful world.

To make matters worse, the priest wasn't done yet. The man was relentless. As if the idea of compelling ourselves to love the guy who started his new leaf blower at 6:40 on a Saturday morning wasn't tough enough, the priest offered a long list of others we were to actively love: the homeless, the convict, the bag lady, the terrorist, the foreigner, the bully who hurts our child, and the thief who breaks into our home. We must do it, he told the congregation, for that is what Jesus calls us to do. And one way to do it, the best way to actively love, is through service.

How do you love when you think you can't? You decide to love and you do it.

How do you serve when you think you can't? You decide to serve and you do it.

Grace and the Attitude of Service

Saying "just do it" makes love and service sound easy and; of course, they are not. At times they are exceedingly difficult. That's where grace comes into the picture. By ourselves, in our humanity, we are not easily inclined to service. Human nature tends toward self-protection. By contrast, divine nature tends toward protecting others, whether or not it is in one's immediate self-interest. Often it can seem impossible to overcome our human nature and act according to the spark of divine nature God placed within us. The odds are against it. That is, if we act alone. Fortunately, we don't have to. Grace is our bit of divine nature, our little bit—as it were—of heaven. Grace is God's way of making it possible to accept His invitation to serve, and grace is what gives us the knowledge that God will protect us and guide us as we serve. The wonderful thing about grace is that it's ours for the asking, and with grace, practice makes perfect. The more we seek and open ourselves to grace, the easier it will become to accept and trust grace in our lives.

Christians are not called to lives of ease. The good news is that grace, love, and service are all connected; they flow into each other, and accepting one makes it easier to do the others. To serve, we must first awaken to an attitude of service. In so doing, we come to recognize that to live our faith, to live our love for God, we must serve one another; and included in that "one another" are those most in need and, sometimes, those who can seem unpleasant or disconcerting to be around. Jesus tells us that whatever we do to the least member of His family, we do to him, and quite often, the least of His family, our family, are people we may want to avoid because they are dirty, unattractive, drunk, mentally ill, cranky, demanding, incarcerated, sad, or angry.

All this is not to say that one's first foray into Christian service should be pitching a bible study class to violent gang members. Relying on grace and learning to serve is a process. The first step is to acknowledge and accept the call to serve as an invitation from God to be transformed. For some, this will be a difficult step. It may be the most difficult step of all, because accepting the call to service means recognizing Jesus as a teacher who wants us to do more than listen to His word. He wants us to respond and to grow.

Saint Paul

Saint Paul is a perfect example of how difficult it can be to receive Jesus' call to service, and how dramatically God may intervene in our lives to get our attention. As a young man, Saint Paul was a pious, educated Jew who rejected the followers of Jesus and their message of His crucifixion, resurrection, and ascension. Not content with personally rejecting Jesus, Paul became determined to persecute and even kill all those who would claim Jesus as Lord. A zealous Jew who considered Jesus and early Christianity a threat to Judaism and the very survival of the occupied Israel, Paul had the authority to obtain the power and the charisma to accuse, hunt, arrest, harass, and, in some cases, order or oversee the execution of Christ's disciples. He was doing just that when Jesus decided to help Paul develop a different attitude to service. Paul thought he was serving God by doing what he was doing, and therefore he was unlikely to convert on his own. Paul saw no reason to change, just as we often think we're doing just fine in our relationship with God. Paul was not seeking grace; he was seeking affirmation of his own righteousness.

To assist Paul in altering this attitude, Jesus waited until Paul was blithely doing what he thought he should do: he was on his way to arrest and imprison Jesus' disciples in Damascus. On the road to Damascus, the spirit of Jesus approached Paul and in a flash of light, threw him to the ground. Groveling about in the dirt, the great and learned Paul found himself blinded by the light of the Lord and chastised by Jesus for rejecting Him and persecuting His followers. Jesus let Paul know that everything Paul had been doing was wrong.

But that wasn't the end of the story for Paul. Jesus made it clear to Paul that he had been chosen to serve God starting at that moment. Paul was shaken, ill, blinded, lying in the dirt. And that's where and when his service began. That's the moment when he realized he needed God's grace to accept Jesus' invitation. In Paul's first steps on the path to service, he had to be led by the hand because he couldn't see. He had to be supported by friends and colleagues because he was too frail to walk or ride on his own. He had to be healed of his physical and emotional weakness. He had to wait for God to make him strong enough to act. All this Jesus did for Paul, who went on to be among Jesus' greatest and most loving servants.

Our conversion to an attitude of love and service will probably not be as traumatic as Saint Paul's, but it doesn't mean we aren't called. And it doesn't mean we won't be surprised by the unexpected ways in which the Lord may demonstrate his desire for us to follow, love, and serve. An important thing to remember about Saint Paul—something that may apply to each of us—is that he had no idea he was on the wrong path. He was complacent, confident that he knew what was right and what was wrong. Some of us may be like Saint Paul: in receiving, recognizing, and responding to Jesus' call to start or increase our service, we will be profoundly challenged and profoundly changed. It may not happen in an instant or through a miracle as it did with Saint Paul, but it will happen.

For me, the conscious process of learning to serve began when someone climbed the wall of my apartment building and broke into my third-floor bedroom window. At the time, I was living in what was euphemistically termed "a developing neighborhood" in Hartford, Connecticut, where break-ins were not uncommon. I'd been away for a week in the middle of August, and the combination of the summer city–heat, my evident absence, and a need for drugs or money had proved too tempting for someone. How this person had managed to climb up to the third floor of my brick building without being seen in a crowded neighborhood is still beyond me. I told a friend later, after I called the police, "Spiderman broke into my apartment."

She wasn't amused. I wasn't either; but for some reason, I also wasn't panicked. I was a single woman in my early thirties living in a tough neighborhood, and looking back, I guess I should have been terrified. But instead I went out to dinner, came home, unpacked my suitcase from the trip, and went to sleep. I know now what I didn't begin to understand then: God was leading me by the hand. Grace was at work.

Gradually, I found myself feeling a little sorry for the thief. He or she hadn't gotten much of a haul. I just didn't have much: books, a small black-and-white TV, an old stereo, Christmas ornaments, and a computer so outdated it might as well have been a typewriter. All of these were passed over with what I imagine must have been a great deal of disdain. He or she went to all that trouble scaling the wall, only to discover such meager pickings. How disappointing!

He or she ended up grabbing my jewelry box, which did hold my few treasures, though even these were of more sentimental than financial value. I was particularly sorry to lose the crosses I'd received at my first Communion and Confirmation, and my beloved grandfather's old watch which had stopped the day he died. I dutifully met with a police officer the next day and he dutifully told me that the chances of recovering anything were nil. Still, I filled out a statement and gave it to the officer and my insurance agent.

Wake-up Call

Everyone, from the policeman to my friends, expected me to put my place on the market—or at least rent it out—and move to a better neighborhood; but honestly, that thought never occurred to me—not even a couple of weeks later when

I passed a young woman walking down the street . . . wearing one of my necklaces. "Maybe it just looks like mine," I told myself, as I kept walking.

"How much does it matter, really?" I thought, as she strode by, oblivious to the fact that she was passing (maybe) the owner of her new trinket. I was strangely content for her to have it. If asked why at the time, I might have said something like, "It's just a piece of jewelry," or "She probably needs it more than me." I might even have said something flip like, "It looks better on her than it did on me." The larger truth was that I didn't mind about the necklace for the same reason that I wouldn't abandon my home and leave my neighborhood: something in me felt the need to live among people who didn't have what I had—white skin, strong parents, an education, and a decent job—even if that meant giving up some of what I had.

That something in me, I believe, was the Lord's voice inviting me to accept grace. And the break-in was His way of taking what had been a vague inclination and transforming it into a map that led me to the first step on a path I'd never have had the courage to deliberately choose on my own.

Was that break-in my road to Damascus? Hardly. It was nowhere near that dramatic, but the Lord does this for us all the time: nudges, whispers, quietly shows us ways to live more fully as His children. Sometimes we are not open to recognizing these loving gestures as grace moments, and life goes on, unchanged. We may take these opportunities for transformation and turn them to our own devices. We rationalize, resist, avoid, and procrastinate. Fortunately for us, God is patient.

Up until the burglary, I'd been lazy about following Jesus' guidance. One reason I'd purchased a condo in a troubled urban neighborhood was that I half believed it freed me from needing to do anything else in terms of volunteerism or outreach. I reasoned that by living in my neighborhood I was doing my bit to help the disenfranchised. Wasn't my presence enough?

I imagine God must have chuckled at my arrogance . . . and then sent Spiderman up that brick wall. In a very real way that break-in all those years ago was a wake-up call, a reminder of what the gospels demand of those who seek—or claim—to follow Jesus. With that burglary, God tugged harder on my hand and brought me to a place that is disconcerting for most of us: the place where we have to acknowledge what Jesus asks of us.

Indeed, whether we are Christians, Jews, or Muslims, our scriptures call us to the same ministry: caring for the poor, the stranger, the outcast. As much as we may want to escape that reality, it is there throughout scripture like a persistent trumpet blast. We are not just called to care for those who are disadvantaged in a nebulous sort of way, as in "Oh, of course, I care about the poor; doesn't everybody?"

No, we are called to minister to the people whose existence we may prefer to ignore or know as little about as possible. We are called, specifically, to feed them, clothe them, visit them when they are sick and in prison, and bring the good news to them wherever and whenever we encounter them. Indeed, we are not merely to wait until we encounter them, but we are to seek them out.

The kind of transformation that this requires for most of us doesn't usually happen overnight. It takes a lot of time and even more seeking and discernment of what God asks of us. I'd like to say that the moment I saw my window gaping open that August evening or spotted that young woman wearing my necklace, I changed utterly. I'd like to say that I was like Saint Francis of Assisi, who tossed all his worldly goods into the street (much to the horror of his confused father, a very wealthy merchant who had given his son the best of everything), and hit the road, proclaiming the gospels and aiding the poor. I'd like to say it, but the truth is, I didn't even come close.

Prayer Preparation

I took two very small, very tentative steps. I prayed for the person who'd robbed me, and I donated a portion of the insurance payment to my church for programs assisting the poor.

Prayer can seem like a bit of a dodge to us at times. We pray for someone we dislike rather than making an effort to be friendly. Is it cheating? No way—not if we take it to the next level. Service starts with prayer, particularly when we are uncertain about how—or whether—to take action. By praying, we prepare ourselves for the journey ahead. We accept that first sliver of grace. Sincere prayer doesn't take the place of action; it nourishes us for action. Just as an athlete prepares for a marathon with certain foods and vitamins, prayer gets us ready for the long haul of ministry.

Prayer also can help us recognize grace opportunities and turning points in our life. Without prayer, we may fail to take advantage of what Jesus offers us. I had a lot of praying to do before I could embrace the opportunities presented to me. Clearly, I still didn't know how to truly give because even as I made the donation from the insurance money, I was denying the significance of my action. I told myself that it didn't make sense to buy new jewelry since what I'd lost was more about my memories than my fashion sense. I wasn't ready to take on the mantle, so I shrugged off the act.

The pastor of my church at the time had other ideas. Around Thanksgiving, a few Sundays after I'd made the donation, he was preaching about Christian giving. While I was sitting there, half listening, he began to describe how a young woman in the parish who was far from wealthy herself had donated money from an insurance settlement she'd received after a theft. He presented that offering as an example of Christian giving! I felt the flush creeping into my face while I anxiously hoped no one would know he was talking about me.

My mother had been a big advocate of Jesus' warning against performing acts so that people could see them. I'd been raised to avoid attention. The last thing I wanted was for people at church to know what I'd done. A few shaky moments passed before I realized that no one in the parish had any way of knowing I was the one he was describing. Feeling a bit like a thief in the night myself, I slipped out right after communion, not wanting to face my pastor.

It was only later that night that the full significance hit me: I began to actually think about what he'd said. Could it be true that my small gesture was all that meaningful? After all, I'd only donated a portion of the insurance payment, holding back the rest to pay for the vacation I'd taken. Was it that big a deal? Was I really following a gospel imperative, as he'd suggested?

Discernment

We don't always have clear answers to questions like these. Only God sees the whole picture, and the best we can do is try to figure out where we belong in the frame. At the time, I was just doing what seemed natural and easy. If anything, I probably felt my actions were as much about expressing gratitude— and maybe even trying to ease a little guilt—for all that I'd been given in life. But my pastor's sermon and the questions it raised in me were perhaps the first conscious stirrings that God was pointing me in a new direction.

Could it be, I wondered, that all these decisions I thought I was making on my own—all by my proud, independent self— were part of God's plan for me? Was everything from buying a condominium in my neighborhood, to not accusing the teenager who I saw wearing my stolen necklace, to donating the small sum to church programs for the poor . . . was all that God leading me to a moment of awareness that I was on a journey of service? And if so, did I want to continue, or step right off the path?

Not wanting to take such an unfamiliar path can be a natural reaction for most of us—a natural human reaction, that is. But when God calls us to service, when Jesus describes how we should follow Him, we are asked to transcend a bit of our human nature and take on the work of God who has a divine nature. That can be overwhelming. How are we to make such a tremendous change? Fortunately, not on our own, as it turns out. Transformation, by its very definition, requires us to put ourselves in God's hands, to accept the gift of grace and let Him do the work.

I began to look for answers in scripture, and it wasn't long before I realized how frequently, how unrelentingly, Jesus exhorts us not only to serve and love one another—the familiar—but to serve and love those who are impoverished, alone, strangers— in other words, the unfamiliar. Again and again, the gospels describe Jesus either telling stories and parables about service or directly commanding it. He consistently urges those who would be disciples to serve the poor, and while doing so, not to neglect to serve and love one another.

God Provides

Strangely enough, the story that struck me powerfully as I looked through the gospels did not, at first glance, seem directly related to Christian giving. It was the lesson Jesus was trying to teach us about hoarding our treasures.

> Then he told them a parable: "The land of a rich man produced abundantly. And he thought to himself, 'What should I do, for I have no place to store my crops?' Then he said, 'I will do this. I will pull down my barns and build larger ones, and there I will store all my grain and my goods. And I will say to my soul, "Soul, you have ample goods laid up for many years; relax, eat, drink, be merry." But God said to him, 'You fool! This very night your life is being demanded of you. And the things you have prepared, whose will they be?' So it is with those who store up treasures for themselves but are not rich towards God.'
>
> He said to his disciples, "Therefore I tell you, do not worry about your life, what you will eat, or about your body, what you will wear. For life is

more than food, and the body more than clothing. Consider the ravens: they neither sow nor reap, they have neither storehouse nor barn, and yet God feeds them. Of how much more value are you than the birds! And can any of you by worrying add a single hour to your span of life? If then you are not able to do so small a thing as that, why do you worry about the rest? Consider the lilies, how they grow: they neither toil nor spin; yet I tell you, even Solomon in all his glory was not clothed like one of these. But if God so clothes the grass of the field, which is alive today and tomorrow is thrown into the oven, how much more will he clothe you—you of little faith!" (Lk 12:16–28)

Perhaps this hit me hard because I am a great one for hoarding. From stashing M&M's to hiding crumpled dollar bills, from collecting paper clips in my pockets to buying books and leaving them unread, I love to store stuff away for the future. The ridiculous thing is that I've been known to keep the M&M's until they've gone stale and the books until I'm not excited about reading them anymore. Of course, this is a lesson in itself: when we hoard things, they become less valuable, less useful than when we take the joy in using or, better yet, sharing them.

What Jesus' parable in Luke really teaches us is that hoarding is, in a way, a refusal to accept grace and trust God. And not only is it a refusal to trust in God's ability and willingness to provide for us, it is a refusal to do what Jesus told us to do: give of ourselves and our means to others.

Such excessive squirreling away of our goods, our time, and ourselves, is a refusal to surrender to God. Scripture is a veritable history of God providing for us when we surrender our will and trust him. When we consider the manna, quail, and water provided for the Israelites during their time in the desert; or Jesus feeding thousands with a few loaves and fishes; or

Saint Francis of Assisi building one of the most influential and generous organizations in the world based on what the Lord provided to beggars or mendicants, we see the panorama of what embracing grace and trusting God brings us.

On the other hand, we can see what happens when we block grace and refuse to trust. When the Israelites stopped trusting God's grace, will, and provision, their story became one of famine, defeat, and captivity. When people didn't trust in Jesus, they would not be converted, healed, fed. When we do not trust in God's provision for us, we are consumed by fear and begin to believe we can never have enough. We hoard.

All of this is not to say that trust is easy. It is not our first instinct to trust others or even God, at least not in the way we need to. How long did it take Adam and Eve to succumb to doubt? How long after Jesus' arrest in the Garden of Gethsemane did it take for His closest disciples and friends to flee and deny him? How long does it take us, after a seemingly negative change in our circumstance, to fall into fear and recrimination, or even to question God?

Yet if we are to follow Jesus' instructions to serve each other and *the other*—those who are impoverished and unfamiliar to us—we must make a rigorous effort to trust that God will provide what we need for ourselves and what we need to serve others. We must teach ourselves to believe that God will provide us with the grace, time, energy, money, materials, intelligence, heart, and opportunities to serve.

This doesn't mean we should wait to win the lottery or to have all our responsibilities disappear. Rather, it means that we should look at what we have right now and believe that the resources are already present for service, if we trust God. If we surrender to the truth that everything we have is from God, then we will be able to see that there is a portion of time, a portion of money, a portion of energy that we can give to those in need.

And even if that portion appears to be small, it is the place where we start.

Psalm 23

The Lord is my shepherd, I shall not want.
He makes me lie down in green pastures;
he leads me beside still waters;
he restores my soul.
He leads me in right paths
for his name's sake.
Even though I walk through the darkest valley,
I fear no evil;
for you are with me;
your rod and your staff—
they comfort me.
You prepare a table before me
in the presence of my enemies;
you anoint my head with oil;
my cup overflows.
Surely goodness and mercy shall follow me
all the days of my life,
and I shall dwell in the house of the Lord
my whole life long.

Service Prayer

Father, pour out your spirit upon me so that I can accept the words and works of your Son, Jesus. Let me pray about serving as Jesus asked me to serve. Grant me the grace to serve. Let me discern the opportunities You offer me for service. Let me trust that You have provided me with all that I need to serve You by serving Your people. Thank you, Lord. Amen.

Questions

- Looking back, have there been times in your life when you did not recognize an opportunity to serve others in small or large ways?

- Does your faith in God include the belief that the Lord has provided you with the grace, means, and resources to serve those in need?

Service Suggestions

- Think about someone whose need for help you have not acknowledged in the past. Maybe the person just needed a word of encouragement, or maybe his or her need was greater. Pray sincerely for that person. Pray for the discernment to know what you should do to help. Embrace the grace you need to act. Do it.
- Make a small donation of time and/or money to a person or service organization you have not supported in the past.

CHAPTER TWO

Begin at Home

"So whenever you give alms, do not sound a trumpet before you, as the hypocrites do in the synagogues and in the streets, so that they may be praised by others."

MATTHEW 6:2

Before anyone can do anything to help another, or others, there has to be awareness: awareness of God's desire for us to serve and awareness of those who are in need. We've all heard the saying, "Charity begins at home." Well, so does Christian service. The most important way a child becomes aware of both those in need and of Jesus' instructions to help them is through observation. If a child sees parents, loved ones, and family members helping others, service will become a part of the landscape. To the extent that a family incorporates service into its routine, the children will take to it as naturally as they take to other family activities.

I have a good friend with an eighteen-month-old toddler. Because her husband runs a restaurant and she herself works, she is constantly in motion. She is often doing two or three things at one time—cleaning, watching the stove, feeding her son. She never complains, never acts as though she is over-whelmed, or has been given too much to handle. She just grace-fully goes about doing what needs to be done. The other day, she told me that she had just dragged their weekly delivery of bottled water into the foyer and then left it to check on some-thing in the kitchen. She turned from the stove to see her tiny son dragging one of the plastic gallon bottles into the kitchen and putting it where she keeps the water. He was laughing and chattering to himself as though he'd discovered the best game in the world. She was amazed and, I could tell from her voice, more than a little proud.

She should be. He is learning to serve. It's that simple: chil-dren, especially young children, do what they see their parents doing. At that age, a parent is the best and most obvious model. My friend had no idea she was teaching her son to serve, or help, just by doing what she needed to do cheerfully and in her typical matter-of-fact manner.

On the other hand, just as children absorb grace in the at-titude of a parent, they will also pick up gracelessness. It won't matter if you take your child along when you volunteer at a soup kitchen if you complain for hours before going, grumble the whole way there, and on the way home, act like you've been released from prison. By the same token, if you resent the things you do to help in your family—like picking up after your spouse, putting together a meal, running a carpool, or visiting an aging relative—then your children will learn that service is something to be dreaded, if not avoided altogether.

Many Forms of Family

When it comes to service in the context of family, it must be observed that families today take many forms. There are two-parent families, of course, though fewer than in previous generations. More often today, we see single-parent families; children being raised by aunts, uncles, or grandparents; foster families; adopted families made up of people who care deeply for each other, but are not blood relatives; even churches that act as family for their members. All of these types of families can model service for the children in their midst.

Is it easier for two parents in a traditional family arrangement to teach their children to help and serve? Perhaps, but the attitude and commitment of the adult or adults in the family may be more important than the structure. For instance, a single parent who is patiently and faithfully juggling a number of responsibilities will model service to his children more clearly than two parents who are focused more on status and the trappings of success than on helping each other or others. A grandmother who is raising her child's child is likely to have the experience to know how important it is to both give and receive help. The love provided by dedicated foster parents will spill over to surround children who cannot be with their birth family. Parents such as these are living the concept of service.

Regardless of the form your family takes, if you have children in your life, you are a model for them. If you volunteer as a Big Brother or Big Sister, teach Sunday school, are a member of the clergy, coach, work in a library, tutor, baby-sit, or are a scouting leader, you have an opportunity to steer children toward service. It is both a joyful opportunity and a considerable responsibility. If you are hesitant to take it on, you are in good company. Even the apostles were nervous about children, occasionally driving them away from Jesus:

> But Jesus called for them and said, "Let the little children come to me, and do not stop them; for it is to such as these that the kingdom of God belongs. Truly I tell you, whoever does not receive the kingdom of God as a little child will never enter it." (Lk 18:16–17)

And that's the great thing about kids: while we can be models of service for them, they are models of faith for us. From them, we learn innocently and joyfully to accept Jesus; from us, they can learn how to translate that acceptance into doing the work Jesus most frequently asks us to do: love and serve.

Prayer as Service

It is never too early—or too late—to start teaching the children in your life about service. Yes, it's easier to model service for very young children, and draw them naturally into helping family and then others. But it can be just as gratifying to take on the mantle of service as a family, making the decision together to begin deepening your commitment to God by helping others. Older children may better appreciate the opportunity to be in on the decisions about what actions to undertake.

Start your family service process with prayer. If you are unaccustomed to regular volunteering, prayer can be a good way to ease into the world of service. Begin by choosing someone daily to pray for as a family. Rotate who in the family decides on the day's prayer recipient. At first, the choices may be obvious: someone who is sick, a family member who is troubled, a friend or schoolmate who is having a hard time. After the routine of praying for someone is established, try to give more thought to your choices. Is there a neighbor whom you all find nosy or irritating? Someone at work who is constantly boasting of how brilliant and efficient he or she is? A new priest or deacon whose sermons seem bland or boring? A grocery clerk who is always surly?

Start to pray for those individuals as well. In the context of selecting the daily recipient of your family prayer, spend a few moments talking about the individual. Whoever selects that day's choice can start by explaining his or her choice. Why does that person seem to need prayers? Other family members may add their thoughts about the day's choice. Does anyone have some insight into that person's life? Does the new priest seem long-winded because he's nervous? Is the grocery clerk surly because she's tired from working three jobs? Is your neighbor annoying because he gets no positive feedback at work and so seeks attention in ways that are inappropriate or intrusive?

These discussions of the person that the family will pray for needn't be long or complicated. In some cases, there may be little to say about the person, especially when little is known about him or her. But spending a few moments being aware of the individual in question is important. It helps us to focus our prayer and increase our compassion for others, to step outside of ourselves—and our own needs and judgments—in order to recognize what is going on with another. It will teach family members that service, even in the simple form of prayer, requires a commitment to understanding those in need. Daily prayer and discussion also prepare the family to take on the next level of service.

A key to praying for others is to pray for the whole person, not necessarily what we think that person may need or should do. It can be all too easy to fall into the trap of praying for someone to change, or to act, according to what we think is necessary or appropriate. Instead, try first to pray for God to open your eyes to the reality of that person and what he or she is dealing with. Second, pray to lift the person into God's kind care, asking only that you be allowed to help in any way God reveals to you as appropriate to His plan.

In essence, prayer is a contemplative form of service that strengthens and prepares us for active service. The two go hand in hand, and the power of contemplative service must not be underestimated. Father Joseph Wresinski, who was the founder of the International Movement ATD Fourth World, lived and worked with some of the poorest and most disenfranchised people in the world. He never discounted the contribution of contemplative servers. Even as he worked at the forefront of every battleground when it came to the civil rights of the poor, Wresinski relied on others. He notes in the book, *The Poor Are the Church*, that he relied on the prayers of contemplatives all over the world as he went about his active service. He felt the poor needed their prayers as much as his actions.

Teaching Moments

While the break-in at my apartment described in the previous chapter was certainly a right turn on the road to service, I had long been aware that there was such a road, and for that, I credit my mother. I don't believe she ever set out to teach me about Christian service, but again, she modeled it in so many ways that I simply couldn't miss.

From the time I was very small, I can remember her sitting down at her desk every week and writing. This alone caught my attention because my mother was not one to sit down for very long. But this particular routine had a whiff of importance about it. At some point I must have asked her what she was doing because I came to know that she was writing checks to an organization that aided families in Appalachia.

Now, there's no way a small child in Connecticut could have any idea where Appalachia was, or even what it was, much less how many of the people there lived in abject poverty. But somehow my mother explained it. She pointed to Appalachia on the map. She showed me the pictures of the children that the organization she donated to had sent her. She read me their stories. She told me about the food and clothing and teachers that her contributions would help support. I remember being stunned! Here were children who were just like me, except instead of eating three full meals—plus snacks—every day, they were lucky to get one. Instead of having clean and relatively new clothes, they wore rags—year after year. Instead of living in warm homes, well-lit against the long, cold winter nights, they had homes with no electricity and no cleanly painted white radiators throwing off comforting waves of heat. Instead of lining up in freshly pressed uniforms every morning to march inside St. John's School behind Sister Theresa like my sister and I did, these kids hardly ever went to school, and they certainly didn't have a hot lunch served up by Mrs. Emmanuelson and her cheerful volunteers.

I wanted to tell everyone—not just about the kids in Appalachia but about what my mom was doing to help them. But she cautioned me. When you give something to someone, especially someone in need, "never let the right hand know what the left hand is doing, never mind brag about it to others." She was stern about this, and years passed before I realized that she was quoting Jesus. I think with my mother, this was more about "not blowing your own horn" (another unwitting and slightly altered Jesus quote!), but it also served the important purpose of allowing those who received her gifts and contributions to retain a sense of dignity and self-esteem.

Giving—whether it is time or money or assistance—should always seek to elevate those receiving the service. Again, we return to grace and an attitude of service. Children should learn, hopefully from example as I did from my mother, that people in need are not wretched, lower forms of humanity deserving our pity and barely disguised disdain. Serving is not something we do to relieve ourselves from the vague bad taste left in our mouths by the idea of poverty, ignorance, starvation, and destitution. Christian service is not an "out" from the need for compassion, respect, and understanding. To the contrary, service should strengthen these responses to people in need, just as these responses should feed the desire to be of service.

Another place where I learned to serve was in school. At my Catholic grammar school, during Sunday school, and later CCD classes, we were taught to visit the sick, help children who were victims of terrible natural disasters in other countries, and be of assistance to the adults in our families. We visited convalescent homes and put on concerts for the residents. The residents may not have thought that our concerts were a gift—considering our untrained voices—but what we lacked in talent we made up in volume! We took our UNICEF boxes along on Halloween forays, put some of our allowances into Operation Rice Bowl every Lent, and held bake sales and talent shows for starving kids in Ethiopia, and what was then Biafra. The opportunities we were given to learn service ranged from helping out in our own backyard to sending food to children and families in countries most of us couldn't find on a map, and would never visit.

Many public and secular private schools are following the example of parochial schools and Sunday school classes by giving students the option to serve in their communities and civic institutions. If your child's school does not have some service component, offer to help get one established, and try to find like-minded adults to support you. Some schools even make service a requirement for graduation. But the lesson is probably better taught by making service voluntary while providing incentives for students, especially teens. My husband and I were working at a soup kitchen near our home in New London when a gaggle of teenagers straggled in, looking bored and a bit resentful. It turned out they had to complete a certain number of hours of community service to pass a class. One young man, with a number of piercings in places that made me cringe just to think about, grumbled to his equally adorned girlfriend, "I thought community service was for criminals."

This is not exactly the attitude to serving that anyone should be aiming for. But interestingly enough, by the end of those ninety minutes, the kids were all a bit awed by both their fellow volunteers and the people who'd lined up for a meal. The ages of our guests ranged from a five-year-old boy, for whom one of the no-longer-sullen teens offered to make a peanut butter sandwich; to a seventy-eight-year-old diabetic who couldn't eat 75 percent of what was offered that day. There were men who'd never been able to work in their lives, and men who'd spent the day painting houses and doing yard work. There were women who had several children by several different men, and women who had been aged out of their jobs and came for the company as well as the meal. At the prayer before the meal, there were tough young men who swiped their hats off their heads and made the Sign of the Cross, women who fingered crucifixes around their throats, and Muslims who patted skull-caps in place. By the end of the meal, the teens seemed a lot more respectful of both those who came to eat and their fellow volunteers. One teen even came back the following week and for weeks afterward.

A local soup kitchen is just one place where a family can serve the community. Many communities and churches have food and clothing drives, shelters for people who are homeless, and shelters for women and children, as well as hospitals, convalescent homes, libraries, and other institutions that offer meaningful opportunities to volunteer or donate money.

And while my mother and the Sisters of Notre Dame provided me with eye-opening chances to help people outside of my town and even my country, the opportunities for families to serve through national and international programs are much more numerous today. Catholic Charities and Catholic Relief Services, Christian Relief Services, UNICEF, CARE, the Red Cross, Doctors Without Borders, Heifer International, and Oxfam are just a few of the major nonprofit organizations aiding people all over America and the world. A family need not spend much time watching the news to learn how many people are in need.

In fact, it would be a good exercise to do just that: watch the news as a family and discuss where and how you would like to help as a result of what you've seen. Whatever one might think of the twenty-four-hour news cycle, one good thing that comes of it is the global perspective it offers on suffering. Starvation in East Africa, genocide in Sudan, tsunamis in Sri Lanka and India, devastating earthquakes in Haiti, China, and Chile, tornadoes in the southeastern United States, hurricanes in Louisiana, oil spills, climate change, war in the Middle East—all of these tragedies and disasters can inform and motivate a family to learn, empathize, and serve.

Saint Elizabeth Ann Seton

Parents and families have a stalwart model of practical service in Saint Elizabeth Ann Seton. Born in 1774 to a wealthy New York family, she nonetheless knew a great deal of suffering and disappointment. Her husband, William Seton, was ill for much of their life together, and she was responsible for both caring for him and raising their five children. He died in the early 1800s, leaving her a single mother.

That might seem to be enough for anyone, in terms of giving: wife of an ailing husband, mother of five children, widow. But Elizabeth Ann Seton had a talent for looking beyond her own needs and past what was right in front of her. Her suffering seemed to increase her ability to trust God's grace. She believed that God had given her the strength to match all her challenges. In the end, she did more than meet her challenges; she transformed them into a life of service that started with her family and community and spread into the world.

In 1808, a widow at the age of thirty-four, she founded her first Catholic school in Baltimore, and the following year she established a religious community of the Sisters of Charity of Saint Joseph's in Emmitsburg, Maryland. The order would grow and support her efforts to educate children all over the country. Being a mother herself, Elizabeth Ann Seton was well aware of the power of modeling service. She did it for her children, her students, and her teaching sisters. By the time she died in 1821, the order had expanded to New York and in the next century would branch out into other cities, and even Canada.

No one expects a parent today to sacrifice as much as Elizabeth Ann Seton did. No one would wish for anyone to experience the kind of suffering and loss she endured. But as we struggle with our family difficulties and the obstacles we face in raising children who will live the Gospel summons to service, it is heartening to know that a woman living in a world that was much more difficult and limited than ours could accomplish so much through grace and grit.

Addressing Challenges

While parents today may not confront the same kinds of obstacles that Saint Elizabeth Ann Seton faced, our complicated world presents its own challenges when it comes to service. These may be magnified if we are approaching the concept of service in a family where the children are older. Preparing for service seems simple in theory—discussion, awareness, prayer, selecting an action; however, in the reality of our crammed-full world, implementing a family service plan can seem impossible.

Do the adults really have time to discuss and model service when they barely have time to open the mail? How can children who have to be begged to coherently describe one single thing about their day be lured into the process of becoming servants? What if there is disagreement about what form service should take? What if someone can't be convinced that helping others is a Gospel imperative and necessary to keeping the spark of the divine alive? What if family members have different ideas about how much to give of themselves and their time?

These are all very real concerns. But serving one another and others is a valid objective. A close reading of the gospels suggests it may be the most valid thing we can do to meet Jesus where He stood and where He stands. Addressing the challenges to service in the context of family is a form of service in and of itself. To confront and deal with these difficulties is an affirmation of service, a way of signaling that helping others is central to the meaning and the heart of family.

Should anyone be forced into serving? Probably not. If a family member simply won't become involved, or if service is a new concept that someone strongly rejects, compromise may be in order. Those who feel ready and able to pray for, and help, others should proceed; in this case, actions will truly speak louder than words. If someone you love doesn't want to join you in service, he or she won't be able to avoid knowing and observing you serving. To the extent that the unwilling individual or individuals experience service through you and other family members, they will inevitably be impacted. And, as with the parent modeling service to a small child, an attitude of commitment and good cheer is essential to show the reluctant family member(s) the vitality and spirit inherent in helping others.

Several years ago when my husband was working ninety-hour weeks and barely had time for a trip to Home Depot on the weekend, we finally got away and spent some time in northern California—Charlie's favorite place in the world. Still, he worked on his computer and cell phone every day, though we were supposed to be relaxing. As we were driving through San Francisco one afternoon, I saw an elderly man, a street person, hunched against a brick wall on the sidewalk. Traffic was congested and slow, and as we passed, his eyes met mine. I kept quiet; I knew the last thing Charlie would want to do would be to try to stop, or worse, turn the car around in such traffic. Plus, this drive through the city had been one time he'd truly left work behind and was enjoying himself. I didn't want to put a dent in his pleasure.

But I couldn't stand it, and after we'd gone a few hundred yards, I asked, "Do you have any money? I'd like to go back and give that guy something."

Now Charlie is basically an angel. However, at that point in our life together, he had not come to share my habit of automatically giving to people who appeared to be in need. Like many people, and I daresay especially men, he tended to look upon some street people as scammers and he didn't want to be played for a fool. So, that afternoon in San Francisco, he said with just a touch of irritation, "I don't want to go all the way back there. The traffic is terrible. Next time we see someone, we'll stop."

I was silent. I understood. He was being very sensible. Five minutes later he sighed and turned the rental car around, muttering, "He probably won't even be there when we get back."

Of course, he was. I jumped out of the car and handed him a few dollars, certainly nothing that was going to change his life in any significant way. He looked directly into my eyes, and I was disconcerted to see how clear his gaze was. "God bless you," he said quietly, and then nodding to my waiting husband, "and him."

I got back into the car and told Charlie, "He said God bless us."

"Mmmm," said Charlie.

Today, Charlie works less and volunteers more—a lot more. The other day he was rushing out and I asked where he was off to. "I've got to meet the public defender to see if we can get one of the guys from the shelter out of prison by Christmas."

"That's great," I groused, "but maybe some time soon you'll have time for the stuff that needs to be done around here?"

He kissed me on the top of my head and was gone, no promises made. After a few minutes of growling to myself, I stopped short, gave myself a mental smack on the head and started laughing. I was reaping what I'd sown, and in the end, it struck me as a pretty good harvest.

It was also proof that a family setting out on the path of service will face many bumps in the road. Roles may change. The strongest proponent of volunteerism may get more than she bargained for when everyone wants to volunteer and no one wants to take out the trash. The most reluctant family member may find an open door to service with changes in a work routine or schedule. The key thing for families seeking to help is to nurture a core commitment . . . and then stay flexible and tolerant. What you learn from each other in the process will open your eyes to aspects of your relationships and your faith that may surprise you.

An anecdote called "The Pastor and the Post Office" recently made its way around the Internet. A priest who was new to the town he'd been sent to serve, was wandering down Main Street when he saw a small boy on a bike. "Excuse me, son," called the priest, "but could you tell me where the post office is?" The obliging child nodded and rode slowly off, beckoning for the priest to follow. A few moments and several streets later, the boy pointed to a white building with black shutters. "Thank you!" said the priest. Seeing an opportunity to increase his flock, the priest spoke before the boy could ride off: "My name is Father Miller, and if you come to my church on Sunday, I'll tell you how to get to heaven." The boy looked at him with a mixture of disbelief and pity. "Father," he said, "you can't even find the post office. How are you going to tell me how to get to heaven?"

We can tell our children and family about service until we're all talked out. It's what we show them that matters.

Psalm 34:11–19

Come, O children, listen to me;
I will teach you the fear of the Lord.
Which of you desires life,
and covets many days to enjoy good?
Keep your tongue from evil,
and your lips from speaking deceit.
Depart from evil, and do good;
seek peace and pursue it.
The eyes of the Lord are on the righteous,
and his ears are open to their cry.
The face of the Lord is against evildoers,
to cut off the remembrance of them from the earth.
When the righteous cry for help, the Lord hears,
and rescues them from all their troubles.
The Lord is near to the brokenhearted,
and saves the crushed in spirit.
Many are the afflictions of the righteous,
but the Lord rescues them from them all.

Service Prayer

Father, You are the ultimate parent, the parent we all dream of having. Your love for me knows no bounds and Your way is the only way. You sent me the perfect model for service: Your

Son, Jesus Christ. In that, You demonstrated that service is, indeed, a family affair. Whatever form my family takes, let me learn service from those I love and give me the opportunities to teach them how to serve. Together, let us do the work Your Son gave us to do so that we may be more complete members of Your heavenly family.

Questions

- What opportunities for family service are you aware of, both in your home and your community?
- In a society centered on self and stuff, how can we teach our children compassion for the needy?
- In what concrete ways do you try to set an example of service for the young people in your life? Who among your loved ones has taught you about service?

Service Suggestions

- Gather members of your family, whether it is a traditional family or one you've formed, and pray for those in need and for the grace to serve. Discuss how you can work together to better serve people who are troubled, in trouble, poor, and ill. Let each person talk about what he or she has done in the past, is currently doing, or would like to do to serve others. Close your meeting with a plan and a prayer.
- Reach out to a family member and invite him or her to join you in an act of service. Possibilities include visiting a convalescent home or someone who is sick or hospitalized; volunteering at a soup kitchen or shelter; donating clothing or food; or even signing up to be regular volunteers at an organization such as a local hospital or clinic, the Salvation Army, Catholic Charities, or Goodwill Industries.

CHAPTER THREE

Pay Attention

When Jesus came to the place, He looked up and said,
"Zacchaeus, hurry and come down; for I must stay at
your house today." All who saw it began to grumble
and said, "He has gone to be the guest of one who is
a sinner." Zacchaeus stood there and said to the Lord,
"Look, half of my possessions, Lord, I will give to the
poor; and if I have defrauded anyone of anything, I will
pay back four times as much." Then Jesus said to him,
"Today salvation has come to this house, because he too
is a son of Abraham. For the Son of Man came to seek
out and to save the lost."

LUKE **19:5, 7–10**

One of the most wonderful things about Jesus is that He
always surprises us. In the same way that He surprised the people, especially the leaders of those days, Jesus often astonish-
es us by selecting people we least expect and then showering
them with attention and grace. Just when we think we have
Jesus all figured out—ah yes, He's all about the poor, the needy,

the troubled—Jesus reaches out in a large crowd to perhaps the wealthiest man in sight, someone who is, we may infer, a bit shady in his business dealings.

Zacchaeus, we are told, was not just a tax collector, but a chief tax collector. There were few Jews more despised by their own people than those who collected taxes for the Roman occupiers—in part because their livelihood came from taking extra for themselves. The fact that Zacchaeus was rich meant that he had defrauded many. Jesus Himself calls him a sinner. Clearly, Zacchaeus hadn't exactly been an exemplary member of society.

But Jesus dines with Zacchaeus—in fact, it is Jesus' idea to do so! Those in the crowd who considered themselves righteous had plenty to say about Jesus choosing to dine with Zacchaeus. They grumble that Jesus plans to eat with a sinner, but Zacchaeus knows what has happened to him. Adept as he is at recognizing the power of money, he is even better at recognizing the power of salvation. He immediately justifies Jesus' kindness to him by describing in front of the whole crowd how he will change his life. At the moment of his salvation, Zacchaeus offers to pay back anyone he'd defrauded. This gesture by Zacchaeus means much more than simply paying people back—it means the end of his lifestyle as he has known it. No tax collector in the Roman world grew rich by being honest with people about what they owed.

Would we choose Zacchaeus as someone in need of our service? Would we lovingly minister to a rich, clever banker who had taken our money? Would we model volunteerism to a hedge-fund manager who had ruined investors, or would we assume that such individuals neither wanted, needed, nor deserved our help?

On the other end of the spectrum, we see Jesus ministering to lepers who have nothing and no one, people who cling to Jesus with a desperate hope that would be hard to witness if we didn't know the end of the story. We see a hemorrhaging woman, made destitute by her years-long efforts to buy a cure, grasp the hem of Jesus' robe even though a bleeding woman would have been anathema to the Jews. We see Jesus eating and teaching in the homes of the wealthy, as comfortable as when He meets His cousin, John the Baptist, who possesses nothing and survives on locusts and wild honey.

Choices Galore

In the example of service Jesus set for us, He gives us every choice . . . and no choice. We have no choice but to help others if we are to follow Jesus; but amazingly, we have every choice about whom we will help. He shows us that there is no wrong choice when it comes to serving others. We must take care when we set out on the path of service not to let our own prejudices steer us onto a narrow, judgmental, or dead-end road. The road to service is a freeway, one on which we should often change lanes. For some, helping people who are comfortably off, who live in a clean home, and are inoffensive in any way—perhaps even attractive—may be an easier route to take. For others, the call to minister to the poor, hungry, sick, homeless, or imprisoned may be the obvious path. Another group may look for those who are in need in some way, but don't fall into either extreme.

It's all good. While God might eventually call upon us to go beyond our comfort zones, it is safe to say that wherever we feel most comfortable starting to serve is where we should begin. It just isn't the place where we should end. It's fine to ease into helping others by choosing those we are most comfortable with or feel called to help. But that's only the beginning. To live a gospel life of service, eventually we will need to expand the number and type of people we reach out to. Though it may seem hard to believe, it isn't as difficult as it sounds. The very nature of serving opens us to new experiences, thoughts, and beliefs. As we seek out and meet people in need—even those we believe we know and are comfortable with—there will be surprises.

The woman you visit because she is ill and you thought was financially secure, may have serious money troubles that she has kept hidden from others. In helping her, and entering her life and world more fully, you may find you are assisting someone who is on the brink of poverty, the kind of person you hadn't thought you'd feel at ease with. If you volunteer at a convalescent home because you enjoy older people and want to be of help to someone who has no family, you may discover that the family formed by the staff and residents is closer and more accepting than your own. If you offer to help out at your child's parochial school because you want to be with families like your own, you might notice that a child you thought belonged to a "good home" comes to school with unexplained bruises.

On the other hand, if you decide that the people most worth helping are those who appear most lost and disenfranchised, your preconceived notions could be turned inside out. The poor, wretched, death-row prisoner to whom you become a pen pal turns out to have a faith that rivals or even surpasses your own. When you show up at the soup kitchen to help feed the desperate and destitute, you see the man who put the gutters on your house. At the homeless shelter at Christmas, when you drop some new socks and sweatshirts off for residents who have nothing to celebrate, you walk in to find impromptu Christmas caroling more spirited than anything you heard from the choir at church.

Experiences like these make it easier for us to cross boundary lines we never thought we'd dare approach. Indeed, we may cross them before we even know we've done it. Putting ourselves in a position of service is, in many ways, an extraordinary adventure, with Jesus as the group leader, filling us with the grace and the spirit we need to move beyond our initial limitations. Wherever we are in our lives, we can make ourselves accessible to this kind of transformation by paying attention to the opportunities all around us to help others and to meet Jesus where He still stands . . . with all who are in need.

Letting God Choose

Shortly after Charlie and I married, we moved to a pretty little village on a harbor in Connecticut. It seemed too pretty, at least for me; I was accustomed to living in small cities, and the village was almost too picturesque to bear. Everyone seemed the same to me: white, wealthy, pleased with themselves. (It's embarrassing to remember how sure I was of my opinions in those days.) I felt as if I had to do something to recover the sense of community and diversity I'd known living in Hartford. I asked the pastor of the church I attended in the village about volunteer opportunities. I figured he'd hook me up with one of the city hospitals, shelters, or meal centers in the surrounding region.

Not exactly. The priest gave me a short course in eucharistic ministry and sent me off to visit and bring the Eucharist to an older couple . . . who used to live in the pretty little village and had retired to a nearby neighborhood filled with other older couples from the village. I politely agreed, but inside I was thinking, "Oh great, more of the same."

This, of course, was not the greatest attitude toward service. Nonetheless, I scheduled a visit which was, unsurprisingly, awkward. They didn't know quite what to make of me, and I was more than a little surprised by what I discovered. The older couple was not at all like the current denizens of the village. Indeed, I learned from them over the year or two of our visits that just a generation or two before, the village had been a rousing community of families that made their living fishing. It was still home to one of the most significant fishing fleets in the area; but the fishing families, most of Portuguese ancestry, now lived elsewhere. Many had sold their aging homes to out-of-towners who paid a great deal to live by the sea in a hamlet that had suddenly become all the rage.

After a while, our visits became more comfortable, and I learned a bit more about the history and people of the region each time. Soon, they asked me if I would visit the elderly lady who lived next to them and bring her Holy Communion as well. Her family in turn mentioned an aunt who lived alone. When she was briefly in a local convalescent home, I met her roommate, a wizened, hilarious Irish woman who gave me many hours of pleasure. When I wrote about one of my older friends in *Daily Guideposts*, a woman living in the Midwest wrote to me and, after mentioning that she used to live in eastern Connecticut near our town, asked if I would be willing to visit an old neighbor of hers who was ailing.

Many of my older friends have since died, and I've been led to new serving experiences. Yet to this day, I don't really think I chose all those wonderful people. And I can't really say that they chose me. I believe God presented them to me. All I had to do—all any of us have to do—is pay attention to the opportunities the Lord gives us wherever we are and in every decision we make. The reward will be immense.

Decision Making

While God provides many chances and venues for service, we must be aware of them. This requires a conscious effort. We will not find opportunities unless we are looking for them. To that end, we need to incorporate a commitment to service into every part of our lives, every decision we make. The various directions we choose in our lives can dictate how much, or how little, we open ourselves to others and, through that openness, to the experience of service.

When in San Francisco, I read about a successful doctor and his wife—wealthy, well-liked socialites who had everything— who decided to make a brief trip to Tanzania to help out on a medical mission. They returned to San Francisco expecting to resume their fascinating lives only to find that much of what had made it so wonderful before the trip now felt stale and superficial. In the end, they sold everything, went back to Tanzania, and opened a medical facility. Now they live and work in Tanzania for most of the year, occasionally returning to San Francisco and other cities to raise money for their work.

Granted, most of us are not ready to make that kind of decision. But it was a smaller decision that got them started, and it was one they made consciously and as part of an effort to help others. So, we're not ready to move to Tanzania. Are we ready to spend a week there helping on a mission? If not, are we able to donate money to such a mission? If not, could we help arrange a fundraiser? If not, could we send medicine, vitamins, aspirin, or food? If not, could we write a letter to the editor of a local paper making others aware of the good work being done there and the ways they could support it?

Not everyone can take giant steps, but everyone can be aware of the grace God provides in helping us to find our paths to service. Opening our eyes to simple things each day can bring us closer to service. Where do you do your grocery shopping? Is there a store in your area, like there is in mine, that trains and hires people with disabilities or people who are homeless? Why not shop there? Yes, it may take a few extra minutes to get through the line, but this is an opportunity.

Thinking of organizing a tag sale? Instead, why not donate your items to a local Salvation Army or Goodwill store, where they will be sold to people who need a bargain, while the money paid will be used for service programs? Or, you could donate some of the money from the tag sale to such a nonprofit. Better yet, organize a neighborhood or church-wide sale and donate some or all of the proceeds to a service organization.

Planning a move? In California and Connecticut, and probably many places in between, you can hire nonprofit movers who train, employ, and monitor people who were formerly homeless or are recovering addicts or have been released from prison. These employees are often more willing to go the extra mile in providing service than are staffers in for-profit businesses, who might not consider their job a gift. The same choices apply when you are looking for someone to do yard work, snow shoveling, house painting, and other maintenance work. Many cities have organizations or social-service agencies that act as a go-between for people who need work done and people who simply need to work. A phone call to your town's social-services department can connect you with these kinds of programs.

Deciding where to live can make a difference in how accessible you will be to service. While God will certainly give you opportunities to help others wherever you are, sometimes you can serve simply by choosing to live in a community that is service oriented. For example, most cities—even small cities—have some form of public housing. By living in such a municipality, you are supporting a tax structure that helps the poor. And if you feel able to volunteer at a school, library, social services department, soup kitchen, shelter, employment-training center, or hospital in such a city, you further extend your commitment.

Those of us not facing a move may not feel able to change where we live. Jobs, family, or other constraints may limit options. Such constraints do not prevent God from giving us ways to serve. How we live—wherever we live—is the key. Are you a good neighbor? Do you greet people regardless of whether they greet you first? Do you smile, hold a door open, or offer to carry a bag of groceries? Do you ever drag someone else's trash container out of the street, take care of an absent neighbor's plants, bring a meal, or offer to send a pizza to an individual or family that has just moved in or experienced a crisis? Are you a peaceful person, one who allows God's grace to shine from your very demeanor and actions? All these are ways to serve.

Anything that happens in life eventually can be translated into helping others. If you've had someone close to you die, you may feel devastated and empty. You may have also discovered that you are good with those who are sick and dying. You may have found in yourself an ability to comfort those in pain or fear. I have met people like this and I believe they have a gift from God that is made to be shared. Maybe the time will come when you'll consider filling the loss in your own heart by volunteering with hospice or a similar organization. Or, perhaps the Lord will put in your path others who need you.

The list of decisions we make on a daily basis that demonstrate our openness to God's grace and willingness to serve is endless. Can you decide to drive slowly behind the bicyclist who is in the middle of the road rather than leaning on your horn and speeding around him? When you're asked to bake treats for your child's class, will you remember to make something special for the little boy with diabetes? When you're out to dinner and thinking about that second cocktail, could you forego it and put the money you saved in the basket at church? When the annual food drive comes around and the postal service is collecting nonperishables, have you thought about donating food specially purchased for the drive rather than just throwing in the stuff you don't want from your cabinets?

The point is to be aware that everything we do, every decision we make, every way we implement those decisions, signals our readiness to take the next step on the path to service. With awareness comes responsibility, opportunity, and the grace to embrace both.

Saint Francis of Assisi

A model for the many and often unexpected paths to service is Saint Francis of Assisi, one of the world's most beloved saints. He is often depicted in paintings and sculptures (not to mention garden and yard statues) with birds and animals. He is said to have had a wonderful way with all God's creatures; but there is much more to the story of this extraordinary man than the bucolic image of birds lighting happily on his shoulder.

Though he seemed troubled from a very young age by the need to find some greater meaning in his life, Francis Bernardone took some time finding his way to God. He was born in 1181 to a wealthy merchant family and had every advantage, but he wasn't able to simply enjoy his good fortune. He certainly tried to enjoy his wealth, spending lavishly with his rich peers on clothes, food, and a variety of entertainments. In his early twenties, he went to war as a knight only to be captured and imprisoned. It was during this time that it seems Francis began to think seriously about what was missing in his life. It was also during his imprisonment that he became seriously ill. Once released, he had even more time to think about what was missing. What came next probably convinced just about everyone who knew him that his deprivations and suffering had driven him mad. But for Francis, it was as though he were finally paying attention to the choices God was presenting him. He began to study the gospels. When he read that Christ's disciples were expected to bring God's word to the world with no regard for possessions or wealth, Francis chose to reject the life of wealth and leisure that his parents offered him.

The transformation started when a beggar came to the stall where he was selling cloth and material for his father's business. Moved beyond words, Francis gave the poor man every bit of money he had, eliciting mockery from his friends and rage from his father.

However, opposition only seemed to strengthen him. Legend has it that to prove his point, he began tossing all his beautiful clothing and furniture into the street for whoever might want it. It didn't matter to Francis who took the goods. He wanted to be rid of anything that he felt would keep him from living the Gospel message of service with no expectation of material reward. The idea of a wealthy man giving his wealth to the poor so that he could live like them was astonishing to the people around him.

At the age of twenty-five, Francis committed himself to a life of extreme poverty, causing his father to disinherit his seemingly crazy son. It can't have been easy for Francis, yet nothing in his history suggests he found it difficult. His moment had finally arrived, and by all accounts, he embraced it with great joy. He counted family, friends, and possessions as nothing next to the opportunity to serve Jesus and others.

What happened next was even more surprising. Contrary to what one might expect, Francis was not rejected nor laughed out of every town he approached. He did not end up a penniless, wandering madman—far from it. Instead, other young men, many from families with status and wealth, began to join him. They did not see Francis as a pariah to be avoided, but as a leader to be followed. Eventually, the powers that be recognized that Francis had hit a nerve. In 1210, Pope Innocent III gave Francis and his small group of followers permission to live according the Rule of the Holy Gospel. Francis's influence began to grow in direct proportion to his poverty: the more he and his Friars Minor renounced all material goods so as to better model Christ's word to people throughout Italy, the more his following grew.

God was not yet done presenting Francis with choices. He gave Francis the option of becoming a priest, but Francis chose to remain a Lesser Brother, preferring the humility of the role he'd taken as someone outside the clerical hierarchy. God provided Francis with the opportunity to have monasteries where his friars could feel they had something of their own, but Francis chose to keep the order free of property ownership. Jesus, after all, owned no property. God gave Francis the choice to keep his mission small and under control, but Francis chose to let the movement grow like a wildfire throughout Europe, reinvigorating the faith of Catholics all over the continent. God gave Francis the option of restricting his movement to men, but Francis founded a second order for women under Saint Clare of Assisi, and then, a third order for religious and lay men and women.

Unlike many religious figures who lived after Jesus and the apostles, Francis brought the knowledge and spirit of God to the common people, who often were limited both in participating in and understanding their religion. Around 1220, to better illustrate to the people the meaning of Christmas, Francis created a living nativity scene in a cave or grotto in Greccio, Italy. To show people how much the Holy Family had in common with them, Francis placed a straw-filled manger between a live ox and donkey, and surrounded the manger with other animals and people. For the first time, common men and women saw something they could identify with, as opposed to the often-lavish paintings and depictions of the nativity that they might have glimpsed in a cathedral or palace. He also wrote and prayed using the dialect of the region, allowing people to hear and read words they could understand, instead of the clerical Latin used in churches.

Francis of Assisi was not born into service. He was born into wealth and pleasure. Every choice he made led him one step further on the road to service. Eventually, his decisions, one by one, opened up faith and service to millions, one by one.

All the Poor

> Then Jesus said to him, "Someone gave a great dinner and invited many. At the time for the dinner he sent his slave to say to those who had been invited, 'Come; for everything is ready now.' But they all alike began to make excuses. The first said to him, 'I have bought a piece of land, and I must go out and see it; please accept my regrets.' Another said, 'I have bought five yoke of oxen, and I am going to try them out; please accept my regrets.' Another said, 'I have just been married, and therefore I cannot come.' So the slave returned and reported this to his master. Then the owner of the house became angry and said to his slave, 'Go out at once into the streets and lanes of the town and bring in the poor, the crippled, the blind, and the lame.'" (Lk 14:16–21)

Everyone is poor. Everyone is in need. In this parable, Jesus is demonstrating that the Father calls all kinds of people to faith and service. Some choose to respond, some don't. The greater point is that God does not discriminate. Everyone is welcome because God knows something we often forget: we all are poor and need him.

Where God does not discriminate as to who among us needs help, should we? We must follow where God leads us when it comes to service, even when we are uncertain about the results or have no expectations. Several years ago I agreed to do a talk and book signing at a library in a small Connecticut town where most residents were well off, if not wealthy. My book was about anxiety and trying to deal with it through faith. I was surprised at the number of people in the room, and even a little pleased with myself when I finished the talk. As I was signing books, I noticed that a small group of women were not leaving with the rest of the audience. After I'd finished, they came up to me.

"We want you to do a regular group on living with anxiety," one said nervously. But as nervous as she and the others might have been, they were also determined. They'd liked what I had said during my talk and felt they needed someone to talk with and listen to them on a regular basis. I got over my surprise enough to protest that I wasn't a doctor or a therapist; I couldn't advise them about medications or anything like that. Meanwhile, my mind was racing. How would I have time to do this? Did I want the responsibility? After all, I'd just shown up for a simple talk and book signing; I hadn't planned on anything this intense. As I stuttered and stammered my weakening objections, I suddenly, really, looked at them. All of them: their eyes, their faces, their hope that I would do as they asked.

So I did. We met for nearly four years, at least once a month. Sometimes there were just a handful of us; sometimes, like on the first anniversary of 9/11, there were almost thirty. We talked about everything, from illness to death, from fear of failing to living day by day. The women, and eventually men, who cycled in and out of our group ranged in age from seventeen to ninety. There were parents and children, sisters and brothers, housewives, widows, addicts, and accident victims. There were

Catholics, Protestants, transcendentalists, Jews, and even a few people who weren't sure how or where to find God. There were people from the library's small town, people from nearby cities, people who had just moved from other states. There were factory workers, CEOs, teachers, bartenders, cooks, and those who could not find work at all.

What God enabled us to do for one another during those years is precious beyond calculation. And I would have missed it all, if I hadn't made the choice to say yes.

Psalm 41:1–4, 13

Happy are those who consider the poor;
the Lord delivers them in the day of trouble.
The Lord protects them and keeps them alive;
they are called happy in the land.
You do not give them up to the will of their enemies.
The Lord sustains them on their sickbed;
in their illness you heal all their infirmities.
As for me, I said, "O Lord, be gracious to me;
heal me, for I have sinned against you."
Blessed be the Lord, the God of Israel,
from everlasting to everlasting.
Amen and Amen.

Service Prayer

Jesus, Your entire life was service. Everything You did, everywhere You went, every person You encountered, every word You spoke . . . all resulted in others being blessed, cured, helped, taught, saved. Give me the grace, Lord, to bring service into my daily life. Guide my choices so that in all my actions I follow You by helping others. Make me aware of my environment and those in it so that I can embrace the opportunities You provide to show Your love to those around me.

Questions

- Can you recognize ways in which God is calling you to service in your daily life: through your family relationships, your friendships, your work, your community, your church? Are you open to being gloriously surprised?
- When you consider decisions, small and large, about your life's direction, do you open yourself to the grace needed to incorporate service into your routine?

Service Suggestions

- Tomorrow, make an effort to open yourself to service in every decision you make from whether to tip the person who makes your latte, to saying a few pleasant words to the dry cleaner, or giving a few dollars to the person with the scrawled sign asking for help, or stopping to visit a sick neighbor. If you have any larger life decisions to make about work or living arrangements, incorporate an awareness of how your choice will impact your ability to help others.
- Do one small thing today to help another person and weave that action into your daily routine going forward.

CHAPTER FOUR

Unclench Your Fist . . . and Your Heart

But Jesus, aware of their malice, said, "Why are you putting me to the test you hypocrites? Show me the coin used for the tax." And they brought him a denarius. Then he said to them, "Whose head is this, and whose title?" They answered, "The emperor's." Then he said to them, "Give therefore to the emperor the things that are the emperor's, and to God the things that are God's."

MATTHEW 22:18–21

With one short, decisive exchange, Jesus signals a surprising disregard for both politics and finance. In the world He has come to re-create, they simply don't matter. In the new order, the New Jerusalem, the law is love and the currency is service. Neither government nor money can get in the way of serving God. Jesus does not bother concealing His disdain for politics or finance as we have traditionally understood them. His questioners go away silenced and astonished at both His answer and His attitude.

As well they might be astonished. For Jesus, money and politics just don't matter. Such a perspective was—and still is—unfathomable for most people. Later, we hear Jesus tell Pontius Pilate that Pilate has no authority over Him except what authority God has given. Jesus utterly dismisses Pilate, even seeming to pity the Roman leader for his impotence in God's world. It's a stunning moment for Pilate; he is the governor of Roman-occupied Judea! He cannot conceive of having no authority, and is astounded at the idea that the Jewish prisoner standing accused before him does not fear or beg. But even at that excruciating moment in His life on earth, Jesus has no regard for power or money.

What is important to Jesus? He tells us later on in the passage from Matthew. When more Pharisees come to test Jesus, hoping to trap Him by asking which is the most important commandment, Jesus does not hesitate:

> You shall love the Lord your God with all your heart, and with all your soul, and with all your mind. This is the greatest and first commandment. And a second is like it: You shall love your neighbor as yourself. On these two commandments hang all the law and the prophets. (Mt 22:37–40)

Money has no role to play in these greatest commandments. It had no place in Jesus' life other than something to warn against. It is a warning that even today we find hard to hear. In most cases, money (and earning money, and worrying about money, and wondering if we have enough money, and trying to figure out how to protect the money we do have, etc.) plays a larger role in our lives then we may like to admit, even to ourselves. It is hard for us to recognize what Jesus knew: everything belongs to God!

Nothing we have is ours; everything we have is given to us by God. It's not even a matter of ownership. God does not need to own; God created all things and all things belong to Him. The Lutheran theologian Paul Tillich suggests we keep this in mind by starting our prayers thus: "Almighty God! We raise our hearts to Thee in praise and thanks. For we are not by ourselves, and nothing is ours except what Thou has given us. We are finite; we did not bring anything into our world; we shall not take anything out of our world."[2]

Tillich certainly knew how to put a damper on any pride we may have in our possessions! He reminds us in blunt language that everything we think of as ours, even our very lives, are on loan from God. How does this truth coexist with our belief in earning our own way, saving money, being independent? Simply put, it doesn't. The fact remains that no matter how intelligent, successful, wealthy, or clever we think we are in the ways of the world, it all really adds up to nothing when it comes to acknowledging God as the true source of all we are and all we have.

Stewardship

A number of years ago it became popular for the Catholic Church, at least where I lived, to emphasize stewardship, a concept that has traditionally been more familiar to Protestants. The seemingly new emphasis on stewardship was thought by many Catholics to be a way to encourage greater tithing, another largely Protestant term for giving. I admit to being one of those Catholics. When we were told at one Saturday vigil Mass that instead of a sermon we would have a special speaker on stewardship, I rolled my eyes. Why couldn't the priest or deacon just tell us to hand over more money and be done with it? Whatever happened to the good old days when the pastor threatened us with God's displeasure at our stinginess or, if that didn't work, with turning off the heat?

I could tell by the people around me at Mass that evening that I wasn't the only one preparing to be bored and disgruntled. The throat clearing, foot shuffling, shoulder slumping, and rustling were audible. It was as if we were all getting ready for penance without having first confessed . . . all the pain with none of the relief.

A middle-aged man stood at the pulpit. He was nondescript, slightly balding with sandy-colored hair, and wearing glasses. He put his notes firmly in front of him—pages of them. I settled in, at least doing him the courtesy of not looking at my watch. My dad had always timed sermons he anticipated would be long so that he could enjoy winning a bet with himself—even if he did lose the extra time working in the yard or making us breakfast. I wasn't that bad.

But when the man started to speak, he didn't once refer to his notes. He looked right out at us. His voice was not exactly compelling, but I still found myself listening. He talked about how he had started out giving to the church what he thought was expected of him, and not a penny more (like the rest of us, probably). He believed he couldn't afford to do more than that, and when he looked at his middle-class life, his middle-manager job, his three kids, his wife who was already working part time, he felt himself justified in that belief. He set his jaw firmly against any appeals from the pulpit, much like the one he was issuing now, and continued to do what he thought was right.

Everything changed for him with Operation Rice Bowl. One Lent, one of his kids came home from Sunday school with the rice bowl. Like Christian children all over the country, his child announced to the family that they were all meant to give up a little something for Lent and put the money it might have cost into the bowl-shaped box to be turned in before Easter. The money would be donated to children and families who were hungry and in need. And like families all over the world, the speaker's family wearily assented: one more thing to do, one more thing to remember, one more thing to take care of.

But somehow, in this family, a discussion started. The speaker really couldn't remember who started it, but he thought it was his eldest daughter. Why not give up something together, make it something they did as a family: one meal a week, maybe, or an outing? The middle child protested. Why did they have to suffer? Why not put in a few coins and still have what they wanted? They weren't that badly off that they couldn't do both. The youngest child, the one who'd brought home the rice bowl, began to talk about what he'd learned at Sunday school, how it was supposed to be a spiritual exercise, not just giving money; it was supposed to be about honoring Jesus' sacrifice and doing what He said to do.

The man and his wife looked at each other, both sensing that this was a moment not to be wasted, though they weren't sure how to keep it going. So they all kept talking, the parents occasionally throwing in a few questions that they wanted answered, too. What was their responsibility to others? How should they honor Jesus? How should they obey Him? Did these responsibilities, however they were defined, rest on them as a family or on each individual? Or was it both?

There were more practical questions as Lent and the rice bowl experiment progressed. What kinds of things could they give up to put aside a little money for the rice bowl? If they couldn't settle on something that would deny everyone equally, how should they address the likelihood that one family member would be giving up more than the others? And what about finances? Did the children understand their parents' financial commitments? Yes, they all had chores and received an allowance, but did they know anything about the family budget and how charitable donations fit into it?

The speaker said he and his wife were dismayed to discover that their children didn't even know they regularly contributed to church and a few other carefully chosen organizations. How had this important part of their life not been communicated to their children? He told us sheepishly that's when they realized that perhaps donating wasn't such an important part of their lives. Once they'd acknowledged that to each other, they realized the rice bowl experiment couldn't end at Easter; indeed, like all aspects of Christianity, Easter had to be just the beginning.

The speaker told us that as time went on, the family decided together to pay more attention to how they expressed their commitment to God and to others. How could they become stewards of the faith and grace given to them? He said that they began to question their priorities. Did they really need a two-week long vacation, or could they take ten days and donate the rest of the money? When it came time to buy a new car, would the less expensive model do just as well? What could they do with the extra money? These decisions were far from easy; either individually or together, they were sacrificing things that were important to them. Sometimes, especially at first, they decided against the sacrifice.

"But slowly," he told us, "it began to sink in that whatever we gave, we got it back in multiples. And not only in good feelings, but in more concrete ways. We became closer as a family. My kids became better money managers, and better judges of what was important, materially. We all learned to distinguish between what we needed and what we wanted.

"And another interesting thing started to happen, especially to me. Each time I'd give a little more than I was totally comfortable with, I found that I didn't miss the money and wasn't sure why I thought I'd needed it. Every time that I would reach deeper than I thought I could—sometimes than I thought I should—to donate, I found that, somehow, the money was replaced. I know that may sound strange, but really, why should it? We know that God has pledged to take care of us if we do His will. Why should we be surprised when we do, and He does?"

He told about how after making a large pledge to a church project—one that he and his wife weren't sure was practical—he got an unexpected raise at work. Another time, the family had decided to support a food and clothing drive rather than build a patio, only to find that other members of their church had donated the materials for them to build the patio after all. Appliances in their home that should have broken down continued to function way past any logical date for obsolescence.

The end of his talk was as surprising as the rest of it. He didn't end with a request for all of us to start giving more today. He didn't announce that pledge cards would be available after Mass. He didn't turn to the priest and say ominously, "Now Father will have a few words with you." Instead, he simply thanked us for listening to his story and left the altar.

He was not a dynamic speaker, but what he had to say really hit home with me. Hard. I've never been comfortable about spending money, not on myself, not on anything. In modern, psychological parlance, you could say I don't have an easy relationship with money. I'm a good saver, mostly because I don't like to spend and I worry about the future. I think of money as security, and that is where Jesus challenges me.

God is my only security. That was the speaker's message, and, more importantly, it was Jesus' message. It is one I need to remind myself of on a daily basis. And when it comes to spending money on the needs of others, Jesus gives me very little wiggle room. Our friend Zacchaeus offers to give half—*half*—of what he has to the needy before Jesus proclaims that salvation has come to him. The rich young man who comes to Jesus asking what he should do to attain eternal life is told to give away all his possessions and to follow Jesus. The list goes on, and it is not an easy one for someone like me to grapple with. But Jesus is clear: money cannot come before God, and it is to be used to help others.

So what are we to do in this world where possessions, security, and assets play such a big role? If we are to live by the gospels, by Jesus' word, we must assign these things a smaller role, as small as we can make them. We must use what we have—treasure, talent, time—to help others. When we feel worried or possessive, we must remember that everything we have is from God, and so shouldn't what we do with it be dictated by God?

Jesus' words on money are among the most challenging in all of the gospels. Does He truly want us to give away half of what we have to the poor? Does He really expect us to live with fewer possessions, less wealth? I think He does. This doesn't mean He expects us to be instantly transformed, or like Saint Francis, to throw our possessions into the street. It might be nice if we could be that way, but Jesus fully comprehends our humanness. Who understands it more than He who was human Himself? He knows these changes won't come to us immediately. He knows we are frightened. He knows we live in a materialistic world.

Jesus is patient with us. This isn't to say that we get a pass; we don't. He has shown us the ideal way for a Christian to live. It is up to us to make an effort to move toward this ideal.

Intent Matters

We are all familiar with the gospel story of Lazarus, the poor beggar who lies in an alley at the rich man's door and desires only to eat the crumbs that fall from the rich man's heavily laden table. It is a parable with a number of messages, not least of which is Jesus' prediction that people will not believe in God's message even if someone were to rise from the dead to prove it to them.

One of the most interesting explanations I've ever heard of this gospel came from Father John Paul Lobo, an Indian priest who divides his time between the desperately poor and disabled of southern India and American parishes where he serves to raise money for his work overseas. Father Lobo believes that the primary sin for which the rich man is sent to Hades is not that he doesn't feed Lazarus, but that he doesn't even notice Lazarus. He isn't deliberately cruel to Lazarus; he doesn't deliberately starve him; he doesn't hate or scorn him. He just doesn't bother to notice that Lazarus is there, as he steps over him every day on his way out. He ignores the beggar at his door, whose sores are licked by the dogs in the street. It is the sin of willful blindness to the plight of Lazarus that leads to the sin of not helping him, and, we presume, of not helping anyone but himself and perhaps those he loves.

Father Lobo's point was that our intent matters. How we intend to live our lives matters. Do we close our eyes to suffering, sorrow, and poverty and then assure ourselves we are not in the wrong when we fail to help because we don't see the need to help? Is the community soup kitchen downtown just part of the landscape as we drive by? Do we stare right through the guy at the intersection with the tattered, scribbled sign, "Will work for food"? Or do we force ourselves to take note of those who are in pain or need, even when looking and noticing are difficult? By forming the intent to notice suffering and need, we commit ourselves as Christians to trying to address what we have observed. We do not allow ourselves to close our eyes in the face of the Lazaruses of our world.

Saint Katharine Drexel

"God loves a cheerful giver!" How many times have we heard that rather odd testament? Stranger still, it turns out that it's true! Well, to be fair, God loves us no matter what, but it's quite likely that He smiles to see us giving cheerfully of our time and treasure. This is also part of forming the proper intent for Christian living and giving. We have a wonderful example of this in Saint Katharine Drexel, an exceedingly wealthy woman who ended up quite joyfully donating millions to helping people who had been displaced, abused, and enslaved in America. Her pursuit of justice for the most denigrated people in the country, and her single-minded funding of that pursuit, led Pope John Paul II to canonize her in 2000.

She was born into a wealthy Philadelphia family in 1858 and in her nearly one hundred years of life, Katharine Drexel was tuned into the world around her. She took note of the material and spiritual poverty of people of color. She paid attention to the ways in which people of color had been stripped of freedom, property, and opportunity. And after donating substantial sums of money, she continued to pay attention, observing that something more needed to be done when it came to promoting the well-being of races of people that society had left behind.

She concluded that what was essential was involvement with the people. Katharine came to believe that it was not enough to throw money at the problem, so she began to throw love with the money. We are told little about the way that Katherine's family and Philadelphia's high society reacted to her commitment. But whatever the reaction may have been, it only strengthened her determination to try to give back a little of the dignity and freedom that had been taken from the people she chose to serve.

At the age of thirty-three, Katharine founded the Sisters of the Blessed Sacrament for Native Americans and African Americans. Her sisters were dedicated to educating, advancing, and caring for the needs of Native Americans in the West and African Americans in the South. This kind of focus by a wealthy white woman was unprecedented, and yet her good cheer and dynamism attracted many women to the cause. Her first mission school for Native Americans opened in 1894 in Santa Fe, New Mexico. By Katharine's death in 1955, just three years short of her centennial, she'd founded Xavier University in New Orleans; more than five hundred sisters were teaching in more than sixty schools. Based on intent, observation, and interest, Katharine Drexel had cheerfully given twenty million dollars and her life.

Steps on the Path to Generosity

It's not easy to change our ways if we are possessive or worried about money. But it is possible to take small steps to begin that transformation. We may be more comfortable with some steps than with others; our comfort level must be stretched or even abandoned if we are to follow Jesus. But again, He will understand when we stumble, start slowly, even backtrack, as long as we pick ourselves up and keep trying.

Even seemingly inconsequential efforts are worthy. When I was very young, my grandfather would play a game with me while my mother shopped. We would both walk around searching the floor of the shop or outdoor mall looking for coins. Whoever found the first coin, won. It was not exactly the most progressive game in the world, but we loved it. And, of course, if we found money that had a likely owner, we tried to find the person and give it back. To this day, I keep one eye on the ground when I walk, and I've found a good deal of money over the years, each time feeling that inner squeal of delight I'd felt as a five-year-old at that glint of copper, silver, or even that rare, fluttering, dull-green paper. Some of the money I've managed to restore to the owner, some not. After my grandfather died, I always thought of it as a way to remember him and all the fun we'd had together.

Several years ago, as I became more focused on my Christian intent for living, I began to put aside the coins I'd find to put in UNICEF boxes, rice bowls, or even the empty coffee cup of a street person. Shortly after making this minuscule change, I found a ten-dollar bill. Glee ensued, particularly because I was making very little money at the time and the tenner seemed like money from heaven—which, of course, it was. And if it was from heaven, shouldn't it be dedicated to heaven? I struggled. I hemmed and hawed. After all, a ten-dollar bill was quite different from a ten-cent piece; I couldn't be expected to give up a ten-dollar bill, could I? In the end, I donated half of it and kept the rest. That became the loose rule for quite some time: if I found under five dollars, I would donate it all; if I found over five dollars, I'd donate half. Then, a couple of years ago, I was walking along the roadside in Sausalito, California, just north of San Francisco. Out of the corner of my eye, I saw something flutter. It turned out to be sixty dollars.

It was Holy Saturday and that night the Church we attended was having a special collection for the Saint Vincent de Paul Society in the area. The money would be used to help people in the projects just north of Sausalito.

There was a traffic cop parked not far from where I'd found the money, and I actually felt a sense of relief that I wouldn't have to make this decision. I marched over to him and handed him the bills explaining and pointing to where I'd found them. He looked at me. He looked at the highly trafficked intersection where I'd indicated I'd found it.

"Was it in a wallet or money clip?" he asked.

"No, nothing, not even an envelope."

"Do you know how many people pass through there on a Saturday in the springtime?" he asked, and then gestured to the money in my hand. "It's yours."

Oh no. He wasn't going to take it and do whatever police are supposed to do in cases like this? I couldn't believe it. I didn't want it at that point. The thrill of having discovered such a large sum had faded fast. It was too tempting.

In the end, I put all the money into the special collection. We'd been on some of the Saint Vincent de Paul visits and the poor in that very wealthy region needed a lot of help. It was easier than I thought, and, much as the stewardship speaker had described, I didn't miss it, didn't give much thought to what I might have done with it. Since then, I donate whatever I find, regardless of the amount, and I don't give it a second thought.

This may seem like a small thing, a small story. For me, it was big. It showed the progress I'd made over the years in caring less about money and more about God and others. It also motivated me to do more, to give more. The truth is that all of us have something like this in our lives, something that can help us move more firmly in the direction Jesus wants us to go.

I know a married couple who go out every Saturday for drinks and dinner. They match the cost of their cocktails and/or wine with a donation to a halfway house for alcoholics and addicts. It's about more than just the money for them; it's a way for them to incorporate their awareness of poverty and need into their comfort and pleasure, and it's a great way to start on the road to Christian giving. If you enjoy attending concerts, movies, or the theater, donate a portion of the ticket cost—or maybe match it, achieving Zacchaeus's donation of "half of my possessions" at least when it comes to this kind of outing. Perhaps you could donate the money to a camp that takes poor kids out of the city or enrolls them in an arts program.

If you're a terrific cook, contribute the cost of the ingredients for your next dinner party to a food bank. At Christmas, birthdays, or any gift-giving occasion, agree within your family or office to donate half of what you might have normally spent on one another to a nonprofit that makes wishes come true for children who are very ill and their families. Double the amount you would have previously pledged to sponsor someone in a walk, run, or bike-a-thon. (And then pay up!) When you buy special-occasion clothes, match what you spend in a contribution that will purchase warm clothes for people living in a shelter. Put a dollar, or two, or five, into the hands of someone who asks for money. Look into the person's eyes and say, "God bless you," as you do it. Make certain the person knows that you have seen his or her humanity.

Reach out to others in your efforts to be more giving. This will bring more joy into the process and help others make their way on this rigorous path. Offer to host a potluck dinner or luncheon where everyone brings designated food and drink and pays a certain amount per person to get in. Donate the money to an organization you all agree on, and discuss the possibility of continuing to regularly support this nonprofit. You can do the same thing around movie nights, card games, board games, or other friendly competitions that can be easily held in someone's home.

As time goes on, make a conscious effort to maintain and increase your giving. Don't be distracted by questions like, "How do I know this organization truly deserves my money?" or "How do I know this person won't spend the money on drink or drugs?" or "Do I agree with the politics of providing shelter to people who should be working?" Such questions will eventually eat away at your resolve and give you an excuse to walk away from Christ's teachings. There is nothing inherently wrong with checking out a charity or nonprofit through a legitimate rating service, but don't allow yourself to fall into the trap of refusing to contribute until you find perfection. After all, how would you like it if God required perfection before allowing you to qualify for His contributions?

From Psalm 107

O give thanks to the Lord, for he is good;
for his steadfast love endures forever.
Let the redeemed of the Lord say so,
those he redeemed from trouble
and gathered in from the lands,
from the east and from the west,
from the north and from the south.
Some wandered in desert wastes,
finding no way to an inhabited town;
hungry and thirsty,
their soul fainted within them.
Then they cried to the Lord in their trouble,
and he delivered them from their distress;
he led them by a straight way,
until they reached an inhabited town.
Let them thank for the Lord for his steadfast love,
for his wonderful works to humankind.
For he satisfies the thirsty,
and the hungry he fills with good things.
Some sat in darkness and in gloom,
prisoners in misery and in irons,
for they had rebelled against the words of God,
and spurned the counsel of the Most High.
Their hearts were bowed down with hard labor;
they fell down, with no one to help.
Then they cried to the Lord in their trouble,
and he saved them from their distress;
he brought them out of darkness and gloom,
and broke their bonds asunder. . . .
Some were sick through their sinful ways,
and because of their iniquities endured affliction;
they loathed any kind of food,

and they drew near to the gates of death.
Then they cried to the Lord in their trouble,
and he saved them from their distress;
he sent out his words and healed them,
and delivered them from destruction. . . .
When they are diminished and brought low
through oppression, trouble, and sorrow,
he pours contempt on princes
and makes them wander in trackless wastes;
but he raises up the needy out of distress,
and makes their families like flocks.
Let those who are wise give heed to these things,
and consider the steadfast love of the Lord.

Service Prayer

Jesus, Lord, You had no regard for money. Perhaps that was because You knew what an obstacle it would become for us! I worry and think too much about what I have and whether it is enough. Release me from such obsessions, Lord. Help me to turn to You with the confidence that You will provide for me and for others, through me. Teach me to be generous so that money never comes between me and You and those whose lives I can improve with my resources.

Questions

- Do you believe that you worry too much about money? Do you resent requests for help or charitable contributions?
- What do you think Jesus means when He tells us to give to everyone who asks of us?
- Do you believe that when you give money to help others you are creating treasure for yourself in heaven?

Service Suggestions

- Consider your monthly budget, even if it is an informal tally of expenses and income. Decide to give a portion, no matter how small, to someone in need or to organizations serving those in need. Be as generous as you feel you can be. And then, ask God to help you stretch yourself just a little more. Pray for the grace to add a dollar or two to your monthly commitment.

- Treasure takes many forms. Write to an organization that you support financially and thank them for the good work they do. Ask if there are any opportunities for you to volunteer. Pray for their—and your—success in service.

CHAPTER FIVE

Seek Out Models

"So, if I, your Lord and Teacher, have washed your feet, you also ought to wash one another's feet. For I have set you an example, that you also should do as I have done to you. Very truly, I tell you, servants are not greater than their master."

JOHN 13:14–16

Ritual foot washings meant to recall Jesus' washing His disciples' feet, as described in the Gospel of John, have been part of the Christian tradition for centuries; and at Saint Columba Church in Oakland, California, on Holy Thursday night, everyone gets his/her feet washed. And I mean everyone. Both feet. It takes as long as it takes the infants, toddlers, teens, young and middle-aged and elderly adults, to line up and have their feet washed.

Weeks before Holy Thursday, the women are reminded not to wear pantyhose that night, and many people arrive in their immaculate, formal, Holy Thursday clothes . . . wearing flip-flops, sandals, sockless loafers or pumps. Some stride forward, ready for the blessing; some shuffle along; some are brought to the line in wheelchairs, or hobble up on crutches. Babies are hauled in carryalls, little ones cling to their parents' shoulders, teens nudge each other and try not to look awed. The person in front of you in line washes your feet and you wash the feet of the person behind you. The pastor and some others even kiss the feet of those they wash.

It is a big deal.

And it should be. For this is the night that Jesus set for us the ultimate example of service. God washed the feet of humans. It was nothing more (and nothing less) than that. Through Jesus, God—omnipotent, omniscient, awesome, fearsome, almighty—reaches down from heaven and tenderly washes the travel-sore feet of His creatures.

If we were not so mired in our human nature, this chapter could end here. After all, what more is there to say? Jesus already said the only thing left to say:

> "For I have set you an example, that you also
> should do as I have done to you" (Jn 13:15).

But, of course, we do have human natures, and so it is not easy for us to wash the feet of others, never mind bandage their wounds, wipe away their drool, appease their hunger, find them housing, or ease their time in prison or the hospital. These things are often quite hard for us. Jesus knew they would be, so He gave us this example. His example is meant to encourage us when we hesitate to perform a difficult task and to make it clear to us that serving others is fundamental to our identity as Christians. It is no accident that Jesus provided us with two great demonstrations of faith—the holy Eucharist and the washing of the feet— on the same night, the night before He died for us.

Churches Lead

Christian churches have taken Jesus' words and His example very seriously. Even if we never travel to Africa or a troubled Third- or Fourth-World nation, we can still learn from international ministries. Our commitment to service can also grow through our awareness and support of such work. International ministries are indeed a helpful reminder that Christian service is global in nature even as we live it out locally.

Some of the most difficult service work in the world is done by church-based groups. In Haiti, Chile, China, the Congo—wherever there is a natural disaster, starvation, oppression, grief, illness—there you will find faith-based organizations working to ease the burden of those in trouble or need. Our own institutions provide one of the best and most courageous models we could hope for when it comes to following Jesus' lead. Groups like Catholic Charities and Christian Relief Services are always in the forefront when disaster strikes. After the catastrophic January 2010 earthquake in Haiti, when confusion and tragedy reigned in Port-au-Prince, these two service organizations were ranked with the Red Cross for functioning at the best possible efficiency levels.

In small and large ways, from rural American towns to teeming international cities like Port-au-Prince, Haiti; and Lagos, Nigeria; church and church people serve every day in every country in the world. They demonstrate that it is not enough to just agree with Jesus, or make faint-hearted, disorganized attempts to help. No, Christians are charged with the responsibility of getting the job done. From start to finish, from gathering the dollars in special collections to purchasing food, medicine, and supplies at the lowest cost; from arranging for transportation to dealing with the local governments; from staffing the response to conducting follow ups; faith-based groups know they must be the best at service if they are to truly follow Jesus' example. They are the ones living the gospel, as we say in our technologically obsessed age, "in real time."

A real way for us to serve in real time is to support such church-based groups. There are many ways to do this, including donating money, food, clothing, and supplies. It is vital to understand that appropriate service requires determining what is needed and providing it. Sometimes, people who mean well contribute items that are not needed and must be disposed of by the charitable organization. This adds to their work, requiring volunteers to take valuable time from actual service.

The United States based head of a clinic for the very poor in the Caribbean once told me that a woman tried to donate her deceased husband's false teeth to their medical-supplies drive. Try as he might to explain why the teeth weren't needed, the woman insisted, finally growing angry that her gift was not being gratefully received. No matter how well meaning we may be, we must be sure that we follow guidelines and provide what is actually needed—not what we may simply want to get rid of. For example, if a food drive asks for canned goods and non-perishable items, don't bring bread or milk. Not only is that a waste, it provides extra work for those staffing the food collection. If the people running a clothing drive ask for clean clothes for children, don't drop off your ragged old jeans. It may make you feel better to do so, but it helps no one. It is not service.

Another way Christian churches lead in providing a model of service is in their effort to support immigrants. The Catholic Church is particularly present in this issue, arguing for immigrant rights and against discrimination. Again following Jesus' model, the Church does more than just talk about helping and protecting immigrants. It acts, protesting laws that hurt immigrants, and setting up organizations to help feed, house, and politically and legally defend impoverished immigrants while also providing sanctuary.

There are Christian congregations on the border of Mexico and the United States that regularly risk their own lives and freedom, walking the border paths to provide food and water to people who might otherwise die in the desert. One group of people call themselves Los Samaritanos, after Jesus' story of the Good Samaritan, who went to great expense and risk to help the suffering man who had been waylaid and attacked. This, Jesus reminds us, is the very definition of loving one's neighbor as one's self. Los Samaritanos chose to name themselves after the man in Jesus' parable because they knew the poorest of the poor crossing the border, regardless of how little formal religious training they might have, would know the meaning of the name; they would know that the people calling themselves Samaritans would help at any cost.

Churches are a refuge locally as well as internationally. Find your way to any soup kitchen, shelter, and food pantry, and the chances are excellent that they are run by people of faith, and even if they are not formally administered by a church or church group, many of the volunteers will be people of faith. The poor know this. They know that people who truly follow God's word will help them. Whether the church is a small storefront place of worship or a massive cathedral, the desperate and destitute will gravitate to it, often before they go to government-run programs and agencies. In this way, people of faith who serve are mentors not only to those of us who seek to sharpen our service spirit, but to the poor and the ill and the imprisoned themselves. People who are served often become servants to others in need.

I was sitting in a waiting area for prison visits a year or so ago, reading all the rules for visitors. This was my first visit to a friend who'd been incarcerated for drug addiction, and I was nervously studying the guidelines. Show your ID to the guard outside. Show your ID to the guard inside. Make sure you're on the list of approved visitors for the prisoner you've come to visit. Take off all outer garments, belts, jewelry, and leave them in the coin-operated locker. Sit down and wait until you are called, and then pass through the metal detector. Take off your shoes and any jewelry and pass through again. Do not bring anything with you. You may not hand the person you are visiting anything—not a book, not a card, not a note, not a stick of gum or a candy bar, not a dollar. (If you want to contribute money to their stay so that they can buy soap, shampoo, or a piece of fruit, see page 11). Don't touch the person you've come to visit, unless touching has been specifically authorized.

In the midst of reading all this, I noticed a quiet, well-dressed African-American woman. She wore a small gold cross at her throat. She sat quietly in the midst of the chaos all around us— young children running pell-mell through the space, excited or disturbed or angry or happy about seeing their mother, grand-mother, sister, aunt; people talking loudly to each other, trying to be heard over the fifteen other conversations going on; oth-ers coughing, clearing their throats, blowing their noses. The woman sat calmly, her hands folded, waiting as we all were, I presumed, for the name of her prisoner to be called.

I imagined that, like the rest of us, the woman would eventu-ally go through the metal detector after dropping her wedding ring and keys in a little bowl and removing her sturdy-looking shoes. She would then pass through the door when it buzzed open. She'd wait in the little cell while the door behind her buzzed closed, before the door to the mass visiting room slid open. She would then proceed into the room filled with long cafeteria-style tables and folding chairs. There, I thought, she would find her daughter, daughter-in-law, maybe granddaughter waiting at a table, her eyes fixed anxiously, hopefully, fearfully, on the slid-ing door. She would go to that table and perhaps her prisoner would stand and walk to the head of the table where they would be permitted a brief hug. No contact would be allowed once they took their places across from each other at the table, lest there be some hidden exchange that the guards couldn't spot.

I assumed all this while watching her wait so patiently, so quietly, so peacefully. Then, I noticed the pile of old-looking books beside her. Uh-oh, I thought; she's in for a terrible sur-prise when she tries to bring those books in to her prisoner. A real big no-no there. I felt sorry for her, envisioning how disap-pointed she would be when she learned the rules. Must be her first time, too, I thought; although she seemed mighty calm for someone who hadn't been through all this before.

Suddenly, a guard appeared outside the darkened little-window cubicle where guards usually sat. The guard stood out-side the passageway to the cell leading to the visiting area. He looked expectantly at the woman. I realized then that her eyes had been fixed on that spot, something I hadn't thought par-ticularly unusual because we were all waiting to pass through that entry. But this was different. No one was bellowing out the last name of a prisoner who would be waiting inside. The guard wasn't avoiding her gaze with the bored look of someone who couldn't afford to feel much. No, this guard met her eyes across that tense, buzzing room, smiled grimly and nodded once, decisively. She rose, not hastily but with purpose, lifted the books, and went toward the guard. She didn't pass through the metal detector. Her books weren't confiscated. She nodded pleasantly at the guard and proceeded through the entry.

Happy as I was that she hadn't been humiliated by having her books taken, I was stunned. What about the rules? Why had I been told that I couldn't bring to my incarcerated friend, an avid reader, so much as a newspaper article? Once I'd been granted entrance into the visiting area and had greeted my friend, I looked around for the woman. She was in a far corner of the large space, with four or five prisoners. Their attention was fixed on her and they all had books in front of them. I gestured toward them, asking my friend about the woman and her group.

"Bible study," she answered briefly. "She comes here twice a week. Nice lady."

As time went on, I noticed the woman whenever I visited. I spoke with her every chance I got, but more than that, I noticed the impact she had on those around her. The taciturn guards perked up when they saw her, managing an affectionate courtesy that one wouldn't think possible when observing them with others. Even the space she occupied in the waiting area became like a no-fly zone, a breath of tranquility in the midst of the stress and confusion all around her. The prisoners in her group were calm and attentive, unlike the emotional and occasionally frustrated exchanges between many prisoners and their visitors. I later learned that the women she taught received fewer tickets (sanctions for misbehavior), and not just because they didn't want to lose the privilege of Bible study. They were easier to live with, less distressed than the other women.

I myself felt happier when I saw the woman in the waiting area. What could sometimes be a difficult task became easier when she was there. Even if we didn't talk, just sitting in companionable silence, I felt calmed by her presence, her quiet commitment. Just as she had a positive effect on the guards, other visitors, and the prisoners themselves, she lent me a sense of renewal in my own service. She made me feel that bringing church and God to that place was the most useful and vital thing I could do with this hour a week that I was occasionally tempted to spend in more selfish ways.

God-Sent

The Bible-study teacher was truly a God-send to everyone in that prison, not just to the women who cycled in and out of Bible study. Service mentors are not hard to find, provided we open ourselves to seeking them, and to recognizing them. God sends them to us all the time, sometimes revealing them to the world, as with people such as Mother Teresa and organizations such as Doctors Without Borders; and sometimes revealing them to us in small groups or as individuals, as with the woman at the prison.

It is important to understand that God doesn't always put servants precisely where we may expect to find them. Many organizations not affiliated with a particular religion or denomination are also doing the hard work of service; we should not shove them behind a screen labeled "secular" and therefore disregard the opportunity to find mentors within these groups. Remember that the volunteers and staff working through these service organizations may have faith deeper than we can imagine. Even if not all of them share our belief system, God chooses whom to send into service, and only God knows their hearts and minds. Can people do God's work without really knowing God? Of course. God is in and through and above and below and around everyone; those who practice kindness and service and demonstrate compassion are as much a part of God as anyone, whether they know it or not. And we can learn as much from their commitment, gentleness, courage, and strength as we can from religious servants.

Organizations such as Doctors Without Borders, Amnesty International, UNICEF, Oxfam, Smile Train, AmeriCorps, the Center for Victims of Torture, the American Red Cross, the United Way, Reporters Without Borders, the Jaycees, Rotary, FINCA, and a myriad of nonprofits that are unaffiliated with a specific religion, provide us with opportunities to volunteer and learn about service in areas that are of particular interest to us. Along the same lines, we can find God-sent mentors and the chance to advance in service through health-focused groups like the American Cancer Society, the American Heart Association, Jerry's Kids, Easter Seals, the March of Dimes, and any number of organizations that do research and provide help to families living with diseases like cancer, cerebral palsy, autism, developmental disabilities, AIDS, multiple sclerosis, Alzheimer's disease, and other devastating illnesses. Mentors may be waiting for us when we volunteer at hospitals, convalescent homes, prisons, daycare centers, schools, rehab facilities, and clinics.

The people we serve can also become our mentors-in-service, teaching us about their lives and challenges in a way that no training program or book ever could. My husband and I have learned a great deal about local, state, and federal social-service programs, not to mention the criminal-justice system, subsidized housing, and addiction services, from the men and women we meet at our city's homeless shelter. They are our teachers in service, letting us know which programs are beneficial, which are mired in red tape, and which provide a spiritual, caring element with the material help they offer. This has helped us immensely, aiding us in seeking the appropriate services and staff to solve specific problems. The lessons learned from our homeless and impoverished mentors also assist us in recommending service opportunities for others. We had a friend who didn't feel ready to volunteer at the homeless shelter but wanted to do something. We were able to steer her to a program at a neighboring library where she could help teach people how to learn, or improve, their computer skills, thus enabling them to seek and find work.

We would never have known about that library's computer program without a tip from one of our shelter residents.

People in need serving each other also offer tremendous lessons in service, if we are wise and humble enough to observe such demonstrations. I've seen homeless people advising others in the same situation where to find help with employment, food, housing, social-security applications, and mental health . . . all knowing full well that resources are tight and anything one of them gets limits what the others will have access to. In a very profound way, this goes beyond what most of us are willing to do for our friends and neighbors, never mind a homeless stranger.

For example, if you knew that there were a limited number of beds in a nearby hospital for people suffering from the same illness that your spouse faces, how easily would you volunteer that information to a new neighbor whose sister suffers from the same illness? If your grocer only had a limited amount of food each week and when it was gone . . . well, it was gone; would you tell an associate at work about the place? If you really needed an apartment for your family in a particular building, and there were only a few apartments available there, would you tell another parent looking for housing about it?

Maybe you would do all of these unselfish things, but, if you're anything like me, you might not, or you might only do it with a pang of resentment or out of guilt. Yet, I've seen homeless people do this kind of thing for each other all the time. As people seeking or staying on the path of service, we have everything to gain from witnessing such exchanges.

Nurturing Community and Church Mentors

It is not enough to recognize service mentors; we must reach out to them and even be ready to nurture them, just as we wish to be nurtured in our service efforts. Even the smallest form of support can mean a great deal to someone who may be tired, downhearted, or unsure about whether he or she is really making a difference. In providing such comfort and support, we nurture the will to serve in others while reminding ourselves of the many ways we can help.

Supporting individuals and organizations that serve in our communities may be done in many ways. If your supermarket, a local restaurant, or business employs people with special needs, people who have served time in prison, or people from a homeless shelter, take the time to mention your appreciation to the manager or owner. Even better, write a letter so they can have a record of customer support.

If your church is one of the many where only a few people bear the burden of running its many programs, consider ways that you can support those people. If you can't take on a regular larger role, can you offer to serve on a committee, organize a bake sale, do landscaping for the church grounds, help with the summer or Christmas fair? At the very least, make certain to tell the hard workers how important their contributions are to you personally and to the welfare of the church community. When you are moved by a priest or deacon's sermon, don't leave church that day without letting him or her know it.

When a corporation or large business in your area makes a substantial donation to a school or public event, provides the town with space for meetings, opens its doors for a fundraiser, or provides technical assistance or services to the community, do your best to patronize that business or buy its products when you have a choice. Write a letter to the editor of your local daily or weekly paper recognizing the contribution. Show appreciation to anyone you know who works for the company.

It is easy to find opportunities to demonstrate appreciation if we pay attention. For example, libraries are wonderful resources and places of service for everyone from researchers to the homeless who often find shelter and their only means of communication there—thank your librarian, the library board, and the staff. Volunteers and underpaid staff at clinics and public-health service providers need to feel appreciated. Show your support to people who put together ecumenical efforts that bring churches together to strengthen and serve the entire community. Police, firefighters, EMTs, volunteer members of municipal government . . . all deserve a word (or more) of thanks and support. By offering such encouragement, we serve the servants, thus reinforcing the circle of service in our communities.

Saint Jerome Emiliani

> While he was at Bethany in the house of Simon the leper, as he sat at the table, a woman came with an alabaster jar of very costly ointment of nard, and she broke open the jar and poured the ointment on His head. But some were there who said to one another in anger, "Why was the ointment wasted in this way? For this ointment could have been sold for more than three hundred denarii, and the money given to the poor." And they scolded her. But Jesus said, "Let her alone; why do you trouble her? She has performed a good service for me. For you always have the poor with you, and you can show kindness to them whenever you wish; but you will not always have me." (Mk 14:3–7)

Even in accepting service, Jesus teaches a lesson about service. Jesus rebukes those who grumble about the woman's impulsiveness or extravagance. He recognizes that they are jealous of the woman who blesses Him with this ointment and covetous of the money she spent. So, Jesus calls them out. He reminds them as well that they can and should take care of the poor, always. The poor will always be around; the poor will always be in need.

And they are.

Saint Jerome Emiliani recognized this reality, and like Jesus in this case, he modeled service just after he himself received the grace of service. Born to a noble family in Venice in 1481, Jerome did what most noble-born men did in those days—he joined the army and fought in whatever skirmish or war was going on at the time. Like a good number of such noble warriors, Jerome was taken prisoner; but once imprisoned, he received a special grace. After he was miraculously freed from prison, he believed his release came through the intervention of Mary, Mother of God.

Having found his true mother, Jerome began to follow her Son by leaving the army and devoting himself to children who had no mothers. He devoted his life and his money to orphans and other destitute people, including women forced to live in degradation. Jerome was ordained at the age of thirty-seven, and later founded what came to be known as the first real orphanage. He established additional orphanages, along with hospitals and other facilities for women.

Jerome was also committed to mentoring his faith and his service work, so in 1532, he created the Clerics Regular of Somasca, an organization which provided for the education of young men in colleges, academies, and seminaries. He implemented the use of questions and answers to teach children about the Church, thus ensuring that his spirit of faith and service would continue. Considered the patron saint of orphans, Saint Jerome Emiliani was infected by an epidemic while tending to the ill, and died in 1537.

Life Altering

Just as God provided Saint Jerome with the intervention of Mary, God sends us just what we need when we need it, or in some cases, just who we need when we need them. When we discover these relationships, they can fortify our commitment to service and, in some cases, alter our lives. This is one way God blesses our efforts to serve.

Every time I move a little deeper into the world of service, I am rewarded with these kinds of connections. After I agreed to facilitate the group for people living with anxiety and depression, I met a wonderful older woman with whom I became fast friends. It turned out that both she and one of her adult daughters had been diagnosed with in situ melanoma, a cancer that I, too, had experienced. In situ melanomas are the best of the worst, in that they are the least invasive stage of the worst skin cancer. During the time our friendship was growing, my insurance changed and I could no longer go to my original doctor and surgeon. My friend from the group introduced me to my current doctor who has proven to be one of the most wonderful people in my life.

Does God work in mysterious ways? Not always, at least not in this case. My sense is that God works in life-altering ways to bring together people who need to be joined. He provides us with the individuals we need so we can encourage, strengthen, and assist each other. This has happened over and over again in my service life, and I've been touched by relationships that will bless me for my entire life.

Father John Paul Lobo, the priest from India who preached on Lazarus and the rich man, has proved to be such a friend. By simply reaching out to him when he was new, my husband and I gained a lifelong friend who has shown us the face of desperate poverty while also demonstrating a cheerful determination to address such destitution. Father Lobo has also provided us with an extraordinary model of grace, praying even for those who flatly refuse to help him. He has made tremendous efforts to draw people into his ministry even if it's at the level of sending penny candy to children in southern India who have never tasted a sweet. His kindness to the people he draws into service is only slightly surpassed by his love for those he serves.

In the end, Jesus is the ultimate mentor when it comes to service. The fact that He gives us others along the way to remind us of His message and example demonstrates His unsurpassing love for us.

From Psalm 49

Hear this, all you peoples;
give ear, all inhabitants of the world,

both low and high,
rich and poor together.
My mouth shall speak wisdom;
the meditation of my heart shall be understanding.
I will incline my ear to a proverb;
I will solve my riddle to the music of the harp.
Why should I fear in times of trouble,
when the iniquity of my persecutors surrounds me,
those who trust in their wealth
and boast of the abundance of their riches?
Truly, no ransom avails for one's life,
there is no price one can give to God for it.
For the ransom of life is costly,
and can never suffice
that one should live on for ever
and never see the grave.
When we look at the wise, they die;
fool and dolt perish together
and leave their wealth to others.
Their graves are their homes forever,
their dwelling places to all generations,
though they named lands their own. . . .
Do not be afraid when some become rich,
when the wealth of their houses increases.
For when they die they will carry nothing away;
their wealth will not go down after them.
Though in their lifetime they count themselves happy
—for you are praised when you do well for yourself—
they will go to the company of their ancestors,
who will never again see the light.
Mortals cannot abide in their pomp;
they are like the animals that perish.

Service Prayer

Beloved Father, so often I lose my way. I become confused, weary, uncertain about whether I am doing your will; at times, I feel I don't know what is right. I ask you to send me models to strengthen what I have learned from the greatest model, your Son, Jesus. Send me people who are filled with your spirit, and open my eyes and heart to them so that I recognize that they are a gift from you to me. Help me to banish my own ego and stubbornness when I am shown a better way to accomplish your work. Help me to embrace whomever and whatever opportunities you send me. In so doing, let me become a model for others.

Questions

- Can you name people in your life who have modeled service and true Christianity for you? Have you always recognized these people immediately or does it sometimes take more time?
- Do you consider Jesus a model for your daily life?

Service Suggestions

- Spend one entire day trying to model Jesus. Treat everyone you encounter as you believe Jesus would treat them. Respond to people in need the way you believe Jesus would respond. Make all your decisions— what to wear, what to eat, whom to speak to, how to communicate, how to drive, etc.—according to how you think Jesus would decide on each matter. At the end of the day, write down your thoughts. Where were you most successful? Where did you fail? How would you like to change?
- Ask someone whom you think of as a model of Christian service to take you with him or her on a volunteer activity. Even as you participate, observe your model so that you can learn more about his or her attitude and actions.

CHAPTER SIX

Do Not Judge

"Do not judge, so that you may not be judged. For with the judgment you make you will be judged, and the measure you give will be the measure you get. Why do you see the speck in your neighbor's eye, but do not notice the log in your own eye?"

MATTHEW 7:1–3

How do we avoid judging others? Jesus makes it easy: if we take His statement seriously, we'll go through our whole lives showering empathy, leniency, and kindness on others, because that's what we most want to get back.

But how many of us manage to do that? We are, as the saying goes, only human, and too often, our human nature swallows up that divine spark that lives in us and strains to follow Jesus' instructions. Even knowing that we are not to judge lest we be judged sternly, we can't seem to help ourselves. In many cases, we may have to battle not only our own tendency to judge, but also those opinions taught us by our parents and grandparents. Some of us may have been raised with various kinds of prejudice, and though we know in our heads that prejudice is wrong, our gut reaction may be the one we were taught years ago.

Many among us may have been taught to despise and fear the very poor because they're considered dirty or dangerous or crazy. Another group of us may dread the very ill or aged because we sensed our parents' resentment or discomfort when they were faced with the burden of elderly or sick relatives. And some may be disgusted by people who have been convicted of crimes, believing, as we may have been taught, that everyone who is convicted is guilty and everyone who is guilty deserves the harshest of punishments.

The Christian in each of us knows these are wrong-headed (and wrong-hearted) attitudes. We know that there is no place for such feelings in Jesus; He tells us in so many ways. But it can be very difficult to unlearn such ingrained thoughts and feelings. We must recognize these negative perceptions, acknowledge them to ourselves, and be vigilant against them. By pretending they don't exist, we will simply continue in a state of denial. That won't help us vanquish thoughts that may indeed come to us so swiftly and automatically that we hardly recognize the damage they can do to others, and even to ourselves.

It is by no means easy to serve without judgment. Many of the people in need of help are in impossible situations, and their pain and frustration will be communicated in ways that can make them difficult to work with. When they feel trapped, they may lash out verbally, or just shut down, or even give up. Christian servants must prepare themselves by putting aside any preconceived opinions about who the poor are, or who the sick are, or who the imprisoned are, or who the disenfranchised are. Just as we lay the foundation for service through prayer, financial preparation, volunteerism, awareness, and studying mentors, we must also root out any negative perspectives that will immobilize us sooner or later on the journey to service. We are here to help, not to judge.

Compassion, not Judgment

A wonderful model for nonjudgmental service is the Saint Vincent de Paul Society. Based on the charitable work and lives of Saint Vincent de Paul and Saint Louise de Marillac—two of God's most dedicated servants born in the late 1500s—today's Saint Vincent de Paul Society serves the poor and discouraged throughout the world. They provide money, clothes, food, company, references, and spiritual comfort, mostly through a vast corps of volunteers organized in conferences, which usually include one or more parishes.

The society requires a number of things from those who volunteer under its name. They must be willing to support one another and give time to the poor. They must pray together. They must guard the privacy and dignity of those they help. They should be willing to visit those in need, often at their homes, which may be in public housing or challenged neighborhoods. And, as if all this isn't enough to ask, the key requirement of Saint Vincent de Paul volunteers is that they refrain from judgment.

The volunteers must not go into any situation with an attitude of condemnation. When volunteers visit a home that looks like it hasn't been cleaned in weeks, if not months, they don't assume that the adults living there are lazy or slovenly. If volunteers meet a young woman who has several children with different fathers, they don't assume that she is immoral. If they encounter a family ravaged by the addictions of a family member, they don't assume that the individual lacks willpower and doesn't care about his or her children, siblings, and parents. If they meet someone who has no work and needs help with the rent, they don't assume that the person is idle and won't apply for job openings.

Because the volunteers are filled with the grace of acceptance and not the human tendency toward condemnation, they often discover truths that demonstrate the futility of human judgment. For example, perhaps the sloppy apartment was a mess because the single father with two children who lived there was working two jobs and didn't really know how to keep a place orderly—though his children went to school every day in clean clothes. Maybe the young woman who had children with different fathers had been sexually abused as a child and didn't know a better definition of love. The addicted parent might well have been through a number of rehabilitation programs only to fall again when he lost his job and couldn't support himself or his family. The person who wasn't working had applied for forty different jobs and had been turned down because he was illiterate.

The Saint Vincent de Paul volunteers open themselves to such revelations through the grace and lack of judgment with which they approach people in need. Consequently, they are known and welcomed in even the most difficult of situations, and they are accepted by people who might otherwise be dismissed as beyond help. In other words, by the very people Jesus told us to serve.

It can be difficult to suspend judgment when working with people who are in trouble and need. It is not easy to love wholeheartedly and without stipulation. Not long ago a local restaurant owner brought a platter of food to the homeless shelter where my husband and I volunteer in New London. It was late, around nine o'clock, and I assumed that the food was leftover from that night's customers, food that she would not have been able to sell. No problem with that; it was hot and fresh, and we were happy to get it.

She stood for a while watching me scoop out the casserole onto paper plates for the guys who lined up for a portion. After a few moments, she pulled me aside and said under her breath, "Do you have smaller plates?" I looked at her in confusion. She whispered, "If you put it on smaller plates, they'll think they're getting more. Plus, if you give them a large portion, they won't feel like they need to go out and work for the food."

I took a deep breath. Now, it was my turn not to judge. After all, she'd at least taken the first steps: considering the needy and doing something to help them. Who was I to discourage her with a cutting remark? So I smiled and went back to serving and later tried to explain that I wasn't interested in tricking them into thinking they were getting more food than they were. I also told her that many of them had tried time and again to work for the food, but couldn't get a job or make enough money at the low-wage jobs they did get. I wondered aloud whether she was interested in hiring any of them. She went away bemused, but not angry. Grace and the attitude to serve is something that must be shared, if it is to be learned and practiced.

High Hopes, Low Expectations

Whether dealing with uncertain volunteers or the needy themselves, or for that matter, people in general, a good friend in a church-based social-service organization has an excellent philosophy: "Whatever you do," she says, "do it with high hopes and low expectations."

At first, I thought she was being a bit cynical, but I've come to realize that she is simply avoiding the temptation to judge. She works extremely hard to serve the people who come to her for help: intervening in court cases, seeking food and housing, getting them medical care and counseling. However, if those she assists do not succeed or are unable to do their part, she sidesteps the anger and resentment that might lead to judgment because she has never assumed that the beneficiaries of our work will have a perfect outcome. By the same token, when she deals with professionals in other agencies or the government or even on her own board of directors and among her own volunteers, she also shields herself from feeling bitter and disdainful by remembering that every person she deals with is human, and limited, and in a different place on the path to service. She also understands that everyone who becomes involved in service has his or her own experience and agenda. Everyone has a slightly different reason for wanting to serve, and not everyone has sought, much less achieved, a constant flow of grace.

In addition to protecting herself from the temptation to judge or condemn, my friend's high-hopes-low-expectations attitude offers several other advantages. Because she doesn't become angry with people she's been trying to help, she is less likely to push them into giving up—on the process or on themselves. Needy and vulnerable people are often just one more discouraging remark or act away from abandoning hope. By the time they seek help, they have probably lost work, gone without food, been evicted (and then asked to leave the homes of friends and relatives), been arrested, or endured any combination of these difficult challenges. Additionally, they might be mentally ill, injured, physically compromised, or addicted. Many of them simply don't expect the system will work for them. They expect to be judged. They expect to be shunned. They are accustomed to people ignoring them, crossing the street to avoid them, giving them dirty looks, and asking them to leave. They condemn themselves and feel they have little, if any, worth.

Part of our work as servants is not only to try to meet their physical needs, but also to help undo all the damage that's been done to their hearts and spirits. The best way to do that is to take them as they are, to accept them. As my friend in the social-service organization well knows, we can't help with these wounds if we ourselves are aggravated and nursing resentment against them ourselves. She keeps a little voice in her mind reminding herself always that she is dealing with people who are fragile and vulnerable regardless of how rough they appear. In that way, she keeps herself from giving up on them and thus makes it easier for them not to give up on themselves.

Hanging Out with Jesus

> He looked up and saw rich people putting their
> gifts into the treasury; he also saw a poor widow

put in two small copper coins. He said, "Truly I tell you, this poor widow has put in more than all of them; for all of them have contributed out of their abundance, but she out of her poverty has put in all she had to live on." (Lk 21:1–4)

It must have been fascinating to hang out with Jesus! Think of the things we would have learned; after all, as Saint John tells us, we have only a fraction of those lessons in the gospels. But what we do have shows us that Jesus is the perfect model of acceptance, whether it be acceptance of the impoverished widow who only has a pittance, or the rich who give a great deal. Jesus judges none of them. He merely provides a little lesson on who is making the greatest sacrifice.

When we look at who Jesus chooses to spend time with, we can end up feeling a little surprised. If we were able to follow His lead, we'd be washing the filthy feet of weary travelers . . . and eating at banquets at the richest homes in town! We would be loved and sought by both the lepers and the most educated teachers of our time. We'd be attending joyous weddings and impoverished funerals. We'd be with people who had every health-care advantage available and those who'd gone broke trying to get better. We'd visit temples and we'd visit prisons. We'd eat with those surviving on insects and wild plants, and those who were gourmands.

Most of all, we'd learn. We'd learn how to accept people we might never have considered knowing. And after we'd surprised ourselves by accepting them, we'd learn how to serve them.

In Matthew's Gospel, Jesus no sooner finishes ministering to a leper, than He visits with a Roman authority and heals the man's servant. Would we be as comfortable touching the leper—an alcoholic, an individual with AIDS, an ex-offender— as we would shaking hands with the doorman at a wealthy friend's building?

As the gospels unfold, we go on with Jesus, sitting down with a paralyzed man and hearing Jesus first forgive him and then heal him. How often do we stop to talk to someone, perhaps a veteran, in a wheelchair?

We are with Jesus when He pauses to ask a tax collector to join His most intimate circle of friends; when was the last time we thanked our accountant or bank representatives for the work they do for us? We watch Jesus encounter blind men who have such strong faith in Him that He heals them; for those of us who have sight, do we have faith that powerful? We see Jesus' deep grief at the murder of John the Baptist; how often do we kill a little bit of the spirit of our pastor or the other clerics we meet by ignoring or making light of their messages?

We hear Jesus declare in a ringing voice that the life of a man with a ruined hand is worth so much more than sheep that are treated more decently; do we lavish attention and money on pets while turning a blind eye to people? We stand by as Jesus feeds thousands, never once asking whether the people are worthy—of or need—the free food; do we ever put an old can of soup or beans into a food donation box and wonder whether the recipient of our largesse really needs it?

We observe people who are ill and troubled falling to the ground just to touch Jesus' cloak; how often do we pull our coat tightly around us and hurry past a beggar or someone who doesn't look right? We are with Jesus when He drives the evil and sick spirits out of children and women and men who are dangerous and unpredictable; do we ignore or reject any indication of mental illness in those around us? We feel Jesus' love and tolerance for the mother of John and James when she asks Him to favor her sons; when someone asks for something we find inappropriate, do we dismiss their need as arrogant? We sigh in admiration that Jesus manages to consistently love His apostle Peter, a man who sticks his foot in his mouth again and again; how much patience do we have with fellow servants who we think "just don't get it"? We gasp in astonishment as Jesus lifts the adulteress off the ground and gently sends her on her way, forgiven; have we looked gently and lovingly on those we believe do not share our morals?

We note Jesus meeting quietly and secretly by night with Nicodemus and Joseph of Arimathea; how often do we proclaim that anything that happens behind closed doors can't be good? We see Jesus relax and accept the ministrations of the sinful woman who washes His feet with her tears and dries them with her hair; are there people whose tears we label as false and all for show?

What we learn when we hang out with Jesus and those whom He hung out with is that no one is off-limits. We are not allowed to reject anyone: rich, poor, white, black, male, female, sick, healthy, despised, honored, young, old, moral, immoral, weak, strong, intelligent, ignorant, arrogant, humble, courageous, afraid, generous, stingy, clever, naive, elegant, bumbling, quiet, loud. Anyone could be the person God has chosen for you to serve. Anyone could be the person God has chosen for you to learn from. Anyone could be the person God has given you, so that you can become more like His Son.

Two Saints:
Vincent de Paul and Louise de Marillac

The two saints who kindly touched everyone they met and upon whom the Saint Vincent de Paul Society model of non-judgmental service is based are Vincent de Paul, born in 1580, and Louise de Marillac, born in 1591. These two servants of the Lord worked together and supported each other in their joint mission of charity.

Vincent de Paul, known as Monsieur Vincent to those who came to him for everything from material aid to spiritual direction, was born into a poor family, but went on to experience and accept people of all classes. A model for more modern day soon-to-be saints like Mother Teresa and Father Joseph Wresinski (founder of the ATD Fourth World Movement), Vincent spent time with the very wealthy—tutoring their children and assisting them spiritually, and worked with the abject poor—who received kindness, charity, and material and spiritual support from this extraordinary man.

Besides being known for his charity, Vincent was known for his humility, a trait he honed by preaching missions to the very poor and brokenhearted. He spent two years as a slave in Tunis after being captured by pirates, but refused to judge his captors even after he escaped. In fact, it was after that experience that Vincent helped establish the Congregation of the Mission, or the Lazarists, to keep the movement energized.

In 1625, the same year he began to implement his dream for the Lazarists, Monsieur Vincent began to counsel a young widow with a small son. Louise de Marillac decided to become a nun after her husband died, and with Vincent as both her spiritual director and model in service, she eventually dedicated her own life to follow Jesus' call to help others. She soon established the Daughters of Charity, Servants of the Sick Poor, a group of women who ministered to the sick and the destitute, thereby allowing them to stay in their own homes and communities.

Both Vincent and his protégé, Louise, died in the same year, 1660, but not before they had established a paradigm for service that can be seen in Saint Vincent de Paul (SVdP) conferences all over the world. Like Saint Vincent de Paul and Saint Louise de Marillac, who met the poor where they lived and died, today's SVdP members exemplify humility, gentleness, and nonjudgmental service to the most impoverished and vulnerable among us.

Accepting Others

Saints Vincent de Paul and Louise de Marillac both exhibited other skills, which we would do well to learn. They made themselves as comfortable with people who had wealth as they were with people who had nothing. They did not judge others who were not as far along in their service to God as they were.

They accepted people where they were and how they were, and in that, they won more converts to God and service than any amount of scolding, guilting, or condemnation could have achieved. In this, too, they followed Jesus.

Can we? The deeper we progress in our service journey, the harder we may find it to remain judgment-free, especially when it comes to people we feel are not doing enough to serve others. We can find ourselves becoming frustrated with people who seem to have more money and more time than we do, but who appear to do less or even seem unmoved by the plight of those Jesus told us to help. The more radically we are changed, the more impatient we may become with those who don't seem impacted by the despair and denigration of others. How can they not see what is right in front of them? How can they ignore poverty when they have plenty of money? How can they not observe what we are doing and want to follow? How can they enjoy their wealth and privilege with such abandon?

We must be very careful here. It is not up to us to judge anyone; we don't know what is in the hearts and minds and spirits of those around us. We have no idea what God has planned for others; how can we, when half the time we're not sure what God wants of us? We must not become so carried away by our energy for service that we blot out grace and humility in favor of pride and disdain. And if, like Saint Vincent de Paul and Saint Louise de Marillac, we hope to win converts to service by our example, a dismissive or judgmental attitude will have the precise opposite effect.

Remember, too, that we don't know how others perceive us. Do our quirks and problems and hang-ups surface more often and more obviously than we might imagine? Does God allow others to see our issues and challenges and weaknesses? Does the person we believe is wealthy and lazy think that we are nosy and officious? Does the person we think of as loud and boasting in his service see us as timid and unwilling to be a strong advocate?

If we allow ourselves to become arrogant in our service, we undo any benefit that our spirits would otherwise accrue from ministering to others. In other words, we may be going through the motions, but a heart steeped in false righteousness and haughtiness cannot progress in Jesus' most important lesson: love everyone.

From Psalm 33

For the word of the Lord is upright,
and all his work is done in faithfulness.
He loves righteousness and justice;
the earth is full of the steadfast love of the Lord.
By the word of the Lord the heavens were made,
and all their host by the breath of his mouth.
He gathered the waters of the sea as in a bottle;
he put the deeps in storehouses.
Let all the earth fear the Lord;
let all the inhabitants of the world stand in awe of him.
For he spoke, and it came to be;
he commanded and it stood firm.
The Lord brings the counsel of the nations to nothing;
he frustrates the plans of the peoples.
The counsel of the Lord stands forever,
the thoughts of his heart to all generations.
Happy is the nation whose God is the Lord,
the people whom he has chosen as his heritage.
The Lord looks down from heaven; he sees all humankind.
From where he sits enthroned he watches
all the inhabitants of the earth—
he who fashions the hearts of them all,
and observes all their deeds.
A king is not saved by his great army;
a warrior is not delivered by his great strength.

The war horse is a vain hope for victory,
and by its great might it cannot save. . . .
Our soul waits for the Lord; he is our help and shield.
Our heart is glad in him, because we trust in his holy name.
Let your steadfast love, O Lord, be upon us,
even as we hope in you.

Service Prayer

Father, forgive me for my sins of omission. Forgive me for the times I've been deliberately blind to those in need, for the times I've closed my eyes to their want and my ears to their cries. Forgive me for the times I've turned away in disgust and irritation, for the times I've blamed them for their condition and used that condemnation to excuse myself from aiding them. Forgive me for the times I've chosen what the world calls beautiful and easy over what the world condemns as ugly and difficult. Forgive me, Lord, and help me to do better; overwhelm me with the grace I need to cleanse my sins in service.

Questions

- Have you ever felt sorry or ashamed about something you've done to—or not done for—someone? Have you ever regretted judging someone or caused someone pain because of your judgments?
- Have you confessed this and asked God for forgiveness and the grace to do better? If so, have you accepted God's forgiveness?

Service Suggestions

- Write a brief account of a time when you refused to acknowledge or help someone in need because you had an attitude of judgment instead of compassion. Be honest and clear; don't try to explain or excuse your behavior. Read your account carefully and then write what you could have done to help that person. If there was more than one thing you might have done, list all the actions you could have taken. Pray for the grace and strength to avoid this mistake in the future.

- Review some of the actions on your list that you might have taken to serve in that instance. If possible, take action now to help that person; if it is too late to serve that individual, take one or more of the actions on your list for another or others with similar needs.

CHAPTER SEVEN

Persevere

Just then a Canaanite woman . . . came out and started shouting, "Have mercy on me, Lord, Son of David; my daughter is tormented by a demon." But He did not answer her at all. And His disciples came and urged Him saying, "Send her away, for she keeps shouting after us." He answered, "I was sent only to the lost sheep of the house of Israel." But she came and knelt before Him, saying, "Lord, help me." He answered, "It is not fair to take the children's food and throw it to the dogs." She said, "Yes, Lord, yet even the dogs eat the crumbs that fall from their masters' table." Then Jesus answered her, "Woman, great is your faith! Let it be done for you as you wish." And her daughter was healed instantly.

MATTHEW 15:22–28

It is relatively easy to get started on any of life's journeys. When the Canaanite woman first got pregnant, she was probably delighted. Women in those days had one job and one honor: to produce children. So a pregnancy would have been a blessing. Her husband would have rejoiced. Both families would have been pleased. They would have prayed for a boy, but a girl was born. Yet the Canaanite woman persevered. She loved and nurtured and raised her daughter to be a good and useful girl. Some day she, too, would be a wife and do honor to the family and produce grandchildren, hopefully sons.

The Canaanite woman would have wanted her daughter to be well-prepared. But the love and nurturing and training did not take with this particular daughter. There was something wrong with her. She was not normal. She was in the grip of something that hurt and bound her. She could not be the daughter the Canaanite woman had hoped for. Yet the Canaanite woman persevered. She continued to love and protect her daughter. Perhaps her husband, or her husband's family, or even her own family wanted to put the girl aside. Send her away. Treat her as anathema, as a leper, as something ruined and rejected. The daughter, for her part, could not help herself or advocate for herself. The villagers avoided her and her mother. If there was something wrong with the daughter, there must be something wrong with the mother. Or, the mother must have committed some terrible sin to have such a child. Yet the Canaanite woman persevered. She would not have her daughter put aside, treated like a monstrous mistake. She would not allow her child to be rejected. She kept her daughter with her.

Maybe the Canaanite woman's husband divorced her. Maybe his family made her life a misery. Maybe her own family rejected her for her stubbornness. She endured their rage and frustration. She endured the stares and whispers of her neighbors. She endured the suggestions about her own deficiencies, her own sinful nature. Then, one day, she heard about a new man: a preacher, a teacher, but most importantly, a healer. He was, of all things, a Jew. This was disastrous news to the Canaanite woman, for Jews would have nothing to do with Canaanites. Jews held Canaanites in great disdain, assuming them to be racially and religiously inferior. It would be ridiculous for the Canaanite mother to go to the Jewish new man for help. Yet the Canaanite woman persevered.

Ignoring the derisive laughter of all who knew her hopes, the Canaanite woman learned everything about this new man. She found out where the new man would be traveling. She found someone to watch her daughter and then she undertook to find the new man on His travels. When she did, He rejected her. She was not surprised. She was prepared for this. She had no idea that she was part of His plan to teach those who were witnessing the encounter about love and faith and acceptance. She didn't care about any of that. She had an answer ready to meet His rejection. And when He rejected her again, she had another answer. If He had continued to reject her, she would have continued to come up with answers.

Finally the new man was finished teaching and ready for healing. He made her daughter well. The Canaanite woman persevered. Because she did, she served her daughter, herself, and the millions who would learn from her over the next few thousand years.

Persevering in service can occasionally be a painful drama, not unlike that of the Canaanite woman. It can sometimes seem like a long, slow, energy-draining slog. At some point (probably at many points) on the road to serving God through others, we will become discouraged, aggravated, disgusted, hurt, insulted. It will happen. If we are doing our job right, it will have to happen. It is the nature of service—as Jesus asked us to perform it—that people will let us down, whether they will be the people we are trying to serve, our fellow servants, or those individuals and agencies we turn to for help in service.

Everyone involved is human, which means that everyone involved will fall short and sometimes fail. This is why perseverance is vital. For Jesus, perseverance led to His martyrdom and salvation for the rest of us. For us, perseverance may also lead to saving others, both by providing those in need with the material necessities of life and by offering an example that will reveal Christ to those who might not otherwise come to know Him.

Don't Give Up

There was a time in my life, when I was a very young woman, when I was ready to give up on myself. I just couldn't see how to succeed at what I'd undertaken. I felt useless, stupid, trapped in a bad situation. I felt, most of all, that others thought I was pathetic and foolish. I felt alone in a prison of my own making, with no idea how to get out and no one to help me find a way. Then, I had an accident. Whether it was the kind of accident one has when one needs to have an accident in order to bring about change, I can't say. I do believe that God put me right in the place I needed to be to have the accident, just as years later He would put me in an apartment that would be burgled. The accident itself didn't fix my life or release me from the trap. It wasn't that kind of miraculous accident that opened a door to resolution, success, and freedom. But what happened afterward felt pretty much like a miracle.

Flowers and cards filled the hospital room. I started receiving notes (in the days when people had to go through the arduous process of actually finding notepaper, envelopes, stamps, and addresses that weren't defined by @) from people I hadn't imagined would give me a second thought: people for whom I'd baby-sat as a teenager; friends of my parents; and former teachers. It would have been stunning enough if these had been the typical get-well-soon type notes, but they were more than that. Almost all of them mentioned some way in which I'd helped or impacted the sender. I'd had no idea! The result of that accident—on the face of it, not a good thing—was that something good happened. I didn't give up on myself.

It wasn't as though the accident and the notes and attention gave me a brand new personality or bright, shiny sense of confidence. But the fact that others believed in me gave me at least a starting point to believe in myself again. It took awhile before that belief in myself became my own—and not just a result of the good feelings others had about me. But the fact that others cared for me and thought well of me gave me the tiny shred of confidence I needed to start building myself up again. As servants of Jesus, that's what we can do for others . . . and for ourselves. By not giving up on the people we serve, and others who serve or should be serving, we give them a chance to get a foothold in their own lives. Even when they are down on themselves, even when they think they are failures or ineffective, our refusal to give up on them may sustain them long enough for them to start to believe in themselves. Through our love and faith in them, they can see God's love and faith in themselves as His own children. As servants, we can never forget that we belong to God and that our primary purpose is to show God to others, especially to those who most need to feel His presence.

Likewise, when we are ready to give up on ourselves as servants, we can be nurtured by each other and by God's love and belief in us. An old friend of mine, a Sister of Notre Dame, had gone through a severe depression as a young woman. She had doubted everything about herself, from her humanity to her vocation. As she slowly recovered, she felt she couldn't even rely on the love and compassion of others; the only one she felt could love her was God. So she began to enter life again with the knowledge that although she didn't want to do anything for herself, she could rouse herself for God. She began to "act as if." If she didn't want to get up in the morning, she would "act as if" she did, and most days she got up. If she couldn't bear the thought of working, she would "act as if" she had important work to do that day. If she didn't feel like exercising, she would "act as if" a walk was the one thing she needed to do. If she didn't want to bother with a healthy meal, she would "act as if" she cared about her health and nutrition. After a long period of "acting as if" for God, she found that on some days, she actually did want to get up and face the day. Some days, she liked parts of her work. She even began to enjoy a daily bike ride or walk. Food began to hold some appeal for her. Sometimes, in order to not give up on ourselves, or others, or service, we will need to "act as if." This is another way to persevere.

Persecution and Exhaustion

Jesus warns us often in the gospels that we will be persecuted and pushed to exhaustion for our faith in Him. He speaks of this even in the beatitudes: "Blessed are you when people revile you and persecute you and utter all kinds of evil against you on my account" (Mt 5:11). Jesus wasn't just talking about having faith in Him; He was talking about living our faith in Him. After all, why bother to persecute people for something they don't act on? If we do nothing more than think about our faith in Jesus and think about serving Him, we are not following Him. As strange as it may sound, if we feel harassed and wearied because of our service, we should rejoice that we are worthy to be among those about whom Jesus speaks.

Saint Paul frequently refers to this in his New Testament letters. He writes about how he and the other disciples grow ill, exhausted, discouraged, and even endure imprisonment, danger, and martyrdom for the sake of God's work. Most of us will never experience the level of personal danger and emotional anguish in serving Jesus that early church members, disciples, and saints encountered. And that's a blessing. But most of us will feel some pain, sacrifice, or weariness associated with service, especially if we continue to grow in our commitment. In order to make a contribution, we may have to go without something we want or need. We may lose sleep because we chose to volunteer at an event or overnight shelter. We will most certainly feel the pain of political or community-based decisions that negatively impact both those we serve and the service organizations. There will be frustration and even anger when someone we are trying to help returns to an old pattern of fear, addiction, or hopelessness. We could find friendships strained, or even lost, if a friend doesn't agree with what we're doing.

I once lost a friendship because I agreed to correspond with a man on death row; when my friend learned about it, she was appalled. No amount of explaining my commitment and what I'd discovered about his situation would appease her. In other similar situations, we can find ourselves on what some perceive as the wrong end of a discussion at gatherings or parties where most of those present have opinions we can no longer share because of what we've learned through service. My husband and I can no longer listen to people who scorn the poor and homeless because they cannot "make it" in the world.

These are all losses, all sacrifices that are part and parcel of service. The more we experience them, the more we've progressed in our work for God. Persevering and remaining committed to the difficult path Jesus set before us, will not be easy. In fact, we won't be able to do it ourselves. We will need to seek and embrace God's grace, if we are to persevere. Fortunately, it is a gift ever at the ready.

We tend to try and clearly define our role in service, but ultimately it is God who decides. We'd like to say, "I'll do this and this and this, but I won't do that and that and that"; or "After I finish this and that, I'm done!" or "I can give one hour a week to this cause, but not one hour and fifteen minutes." It does not always work out the way we plan.

While living in California, I knew a man who was on a committee to help the residents living in nearby public housing. The committee met once a month and the chair of the committee would assure us that he would do his best to have us out of the meeting in less than an hour. On the rare occasions when the meeting would go a few minutes over, the man in question would rise up on the hour, collect his belongings, and walk out. He was also given to saying things like, "Let's move along the agenda," or "Let's not turn this into a cocktail party," if other members strayed from what he felt was the proper subject and timeline. This is certainly one way to serve!

It is legitimate to set boundaries and maintain them. However, sometimes the Spirit calls us to break our own rules, risk a little more, give what we didn't think we had to give. If the Spirit calls us, and if we answer that call, the Spirit will also give us the grace and strength and courage we need to proceed. Learning this lesson—and trusting it—can take awhile.

Jonah

The prophet Jonah learned the hard way. Chosen by God to be a prophet, Jonah was more than willing to spread the word of God . . . to a point. Jonah wanted to be the one to lay down his boundaries. He knew to whom he wanted to preach and to whom he didn't want to preach. He knew whom he wanted God to save and who he didn't think worthy of God's forgiveness and salvation. So when the Lord asked Jonah to go and preach repentance to the Ninevites—who might well be saved if Jonah successfully completed this mission—Jonah effectively said, "No way!" Or, more accurately, he tried to say those words:

> Now the word of the Lord came to Jonah son of Amittai, saying, "Go at once to Nineveh, that great city, and cry out against it; for their wickedness has come up before me." But Jonah set out to flee to Tarshish from the presence of the Lord. He went down to Joppa and found a ship going to Tarshish; so he paid his fare and went on board, to go with them to Tarshish, away from the presence of the Lord. . . .
>
> But the Lord provided a large fish to swallow up Jonah; and Jonah was in the belly of the fish three days and three nights. . . . Then the Lord spoke to the fish and it spewed Jonah out upon the dry land. . . . The word of the Lord came to Jonah a second time, saying, "Get up, go to Nineveh, that great city, and proclaim to it the message that I tell you. . . ." Jonah began to go into the city. . . . And he cried out, "Forty days more, and Nineveh shall be overthrown!" And the people of Nineveh believed God; they proclaimed a fast, and everyone, great and small, put on sackcloth. . . . But this was very displeasing to Jonah, and he became angry. . . . But God said to Jonah, "Is it right for you to be angry?" . . . "And should I not be concerned about

> Nineveh, that great city, in which there are more
> than a hundred and twenty thousand people who
> do not know their right hand from their left? . . ."
> (Jon 1:1–3, 17; 2:10; 3:1–2, 4–5; 4:1, 9, 11)

Jonah didn't think the people of Nineveh deserved the chance to repent and be saved, and so he tried to avoid helping them. But it wasn't up to Jonah to decide. God had already decided. Today, many don't believe that people who have been convicted of crimes, or are homeless, unemployed, addicted, mentally ill, or illegally in this country deserve a second chance—or even a first chance, in some cases. But it isn't up to them to decide. God decides who is worthy of salvation, and for all any of us know, everyone is worthy in God's eyes. There is a reason that Jesus calls us to help such a wide variety of people: the sick, the poor, the hungry, the imprisoned, the naked, and the foreigner. He asks us to serve all these and more because, as with Jonah, God has already decided.

Jeremiah

Jeremiah might have been called the Prophet of Perseverance. Like Jonah, he wasn't always comfortable with God's assignments, but unlike Jonah, he never hesitated to fulfill them, regardless of the cost to himself—and the cost was considerable. For following God's direction, Jeremiah was ostracized, imprisoned, and nearly killed several times. Acting according to God's will, he denounced, and therefore offended, many of the most powerful men in Judea from 626 BC to 586 BC: forty years of perseverance in the most dangerous of circumstances. Giving up any chance for normal marriage and family—the two things that sustained Jewish society and were necessary to survival—Jeremiah suffered so utterly for God's word that some theologians consider his life a prefiguring of the life of Jesus.

Jeremiah is called the Prophet of the Eleventh Hour because God tasked him with the miserable responsibility of predicting the imminent destruction of Jerusalem and chastising the people for their sins. He is one of the four major prophets of the Old Testament. Jeremiah was in constant conversation with God, just as all who want to persevere in the service of God must be. The prophet was continually reminding God (as if God needed reminding) that he was living in grave danger because of what God required of him. Because he was the son of a prophet, Jeremiah was prepared for the privations of such a life, but it may be fair to say that for forty years Jeremiah suffered above and beyond the call of duty in service to the Lord. And despite his gentle complaints to the Lord, Jeremiah never faltered in serving God's will.

Jeremiah also persevered when he was accused of not doing God's work. There were many Jewish and pagan leaders in those days who did not want to hear what Jeremiah was saying. So what did they do? Naturally, they tried to make it seem as though Jeremiah was not a man of God, because they could not accept the fact that Jeremiah, in opposing them, was doing God's work:

> The priests and the prophets and all the people heard Jeremiah speaking these words in the house of the Lord. And when Jeremiah had finished speaking all that the Lord had commanded him to speak to all the people, then the priests and prophets and all the people laid hold of him, saying, "You shall die! Why have you prophesied in the name of the Lord, saying, 'This house shall be like Shiloh, and this city shall be desolate, without inhabitant'?"
> (Jer 26:7–9)

Like Jeremiah, some of us will be told that we are not doing the work of God, especially when our service makes others feel guilty, uncomfortable, or threatened. We too can do what Jeremiah did in such cases: turn to God and renew our confidence in His righteousness.

Prepare to Persevere

As the Father's servants, Jesus' coworkers, and the Holy Spirit's vessels, we are in the hands of the Triune God. When we choose to follow on the path of service, we give ourselves over to that extraordinary Trinity and receive grace and strength. We can use these and other gifts God has provided to prepare ourselves for the journey and refresh ourselves along the way. Jesus Himself, when weary and downhearted, uses the strategy of going away alone to pray to the Father. Saint Paul often uses the analogy of a determined athlete to describe his work as a servant of the Lord: "Athletes exercise self-control in all things; they do it to receive a perishable wreath, but we an imperishable one"(1 Cor 9:25). Obviously, serving God is rigorous and requires a degree of readiness and spiritual fitness. God gives us opportunities to train for the job in order to build up the perseverance muscles He knows we'll need.

Prayer is the way to warm up for our perseverance workout. There is a constant open line of communication to God; all we have to do is use it. We can pray with words or thoughts or just by resting ourselves in the shadow of God's power and love. The latter is a good strategy when we feel depleted, or frustrated with ourselves or those we serve.

Stretching our perseverance muscles can be simply a matter of learning what to expect from service. When you feel called to a particular direction or service, do some research. For instance, if you plan to join a Saint Vincent de Paul conference, talk to a few people already in that conference. Find out what kind of help they usually provide and to whom. Ask to go along to a few meetings. If you don't feel you are ready for home visits, offer to sort donations, take calls, run a food pantry, or research other resources. Relying on God's grace doesn't mean you shouldn't use the brain and body He created for you.

Go for endurance rather than the quick win. When working with the poor and disenfranchised, the ill and the imprisoned, there are few quick fixes; it is better to prepare yourself for the long haul of service rather than hoping to be the agent of a miracle. The simple fact is you will never be able to do enough. Even when you succeed with one person, there will be another waiting for your assistance. If you help every refugee in Haiti, there will be refugees in the Sudan. If you feed every hungry child in your city, there will be hungry people in the next city. Service is a life-long venture, which requires slow and steady progress with periods of rest along the way.

Nourish yourself during the long race. Stay close to God. Read helpful scripture passages and spirit-strengthening books. Read for pleasure. Make sure you spend time with the people you like and love, especially the ones who make you laugh. Eat and drink as well as you can. Get physical exercise regularly.

The word "perseverance" does not automatically bring the notion of joy to mind. But there can be joy at the deepest level in persevering in service. We can rejoice in the knowledge that we are doing exactly what Jesus asked us in the way He asked us to do it. What greater joy could there be in life?

Psalm 57

Be merciful to me, O God, be merciful to me,
for in you my soul takes refuge;
in the shadow of your wings I will take refuge,
until the destroying storms pass by.
I cry to God Most High, to God who fulfills his purpose for me.
He will send from heaven and save me,
he will put to shame those who trample on me.
God will send forth his steadfast love and his faithfulness.
I lie down among lions
that greedily devour human prey;
their teeth are spears and arrows,
their tongues sharp swords.
Be exalted, O God, above the heavens.
Let your glory be over all the earth.

They set a net for my steps;
my soul was bowed down.
They dug a pit in my path,
but they have fallen into it themselves.
My heart is steadfast, O God,
my heart is steadfast.
I will sing and make melody.
Awake my soul!
Awake, O harp and lyre!
I will awake the dawn.
I will give thanks to you, O Lord, among the peoples;
I will sing praises to you among the nations.
For your steadfast love is as high as the heavens;
your faithfulness extends to the clouds.
Be exalted, O God, above the heavens.
Let your glory be over all the earth.

Service Prayer

Lord Jesus, You told us that those who persevered to the end would be saved. O Lord, sometimes I feel like I'm at the end of my rope! There are times when my daily life exhausts and discourages me, and I can't imagine doing one more thing. I can't imagine taking on one more responsibility. And yet You tell me that it is Your will that I love and help others. Give me the strength to do it, Lord! Give me the strength to persevere in service. Let the need of others ignite my energy. Let me start with small prayers and small acts until I recover my spirit enough to make greater strides on the path You have set for me. Let me lean on you, Lord!

Questions

- Do you think that Jesus ever got tired of serving? Can you find evidence in the gospels that suggests He did?

- God compelled the prophets like Jeremiah and Jonah to serve, often at great peril and cost to themselves. Do you ever feel that the Lord is pushing you to take difficult actions in pursuit of service? If so, do you believe that He will sustain and protect you as He did the prophets?

Service Suggestions

- Consider one service-oriented thing in your life that you'd like to give up on—one that you just don't think you can do anymore. It could be anything: being pleasant to an obnoxious neighbor or colleague; serving meals at a soup kitchen where no one ever thanks you; visiting an elderly relative or shut-in who does nothing but complain the whole time you're there; or helping to clean up your neighborhood or church grounds. After you've decided on your Achilles' heel of service, ask God to give you the spirit to continue in your commitment to this action. Spend some real time with God over this, pouring out all your excuses and exhaustion, asking Him to understand. Then do what He asks of you.
- Invite someone to help you in service. Ask a friend, relative, neighbor, colleague, or someone from your church to join you wherever and however you volunteer. You will be able to share your sacred burden and draw someone else into service: a double blessing!

CHAPTER EIGHT

Accept Grace

Now as they went on their way, he entered a certain village, where a woman named Martha welcomed Him into her home. She had a sister named Mary, who sat at the Lord's feet and listened to what he was saying. But Martha was distracted by her many tasks; so she came to Him and asked, "Lord, do you not care that my sister has left me to do all the work by myself? Tell her then to help me." But the Lord answered her, "Martha, Martha, you are worried and distracted by many things; there is need of only one thing. Mary has chosen the better part which will not be taken away from her."

LUKE **10:38–42**

I always feel a little sorry for Martha, probably because I am a bit like her. I want to get things done, I want to be responsible, I want to take care of things, I want tasks finished, I want resolution. It seems that Jesus is a little hard on Martha. After all, it is easy to imagine that this scene has been repeated time and again in the household: older sister Martha doing all the work and younger (spoiled?) sister Mary finding a reason to sit around.

But that notion is the result of looking at this situation through a very human lens, one that tends to be blurred by petty resentments and rivalries. In fact, Jesus sets Martha straight: this is not about petty familial competitions; it is about seeking something greater than human approval or human fairness. Maybe it would be fair for Martha to demand her sister's help if the guest in question had been anyone except Jesus. But the guest is Jesus. Mary recognizes His importance more clearly than her sister. What household task could be more important than listening to Jesus? Therefore, Mary had indeed chosen the better part. Mary had chosen grace.

While Martha is becoming increasingly hot and bothered, Mary is absorbing Jesus. Seated at His feet, listening with all her being to His words, filling herself with His presence, she is consuming the grace Jesus is offering her. Mary is intent on incorporating Jesus and His teachings into herself. Jesus has not made this visit lightly. He knows what is to come for Himself and for these two women. He knows that they will soon lose him, the dearest and most valuable friend they've had. Jesus is offering them the grace they will need to survive that dark period, and the grace they will need to continue to be His disciples later.

Jesus is not scolding Martha. On the contrary, He feels compassion for her. He wants her, in her own way, to choose what Mary has chosen. He wants Martha to be as prepared to receive grace as Mary is.

Grace is a gift God constantly offers us. But, like Martha, we can be too consumed with our problems to fully participate in it. We don't understand that sometimes, in order to serve, we must allow ourselves to be served. To truly accept grace, we must allow it to be freely given to us by God, and that sometimes means receiving gifts from others. A gift is a joyful thing, but sometimes it is strangely difficult to accept. Gifts can leave us feeling like we owe a debt. They can leave us feeling defensive or even suspicious. This is the case with human gifts and it is the case with God's grace as well.

However challenging it might be to receive the gift of grace, we must receive it. And on occasion, receiving grace means allowing ourselves to be ministered to in a way we do not accept. Just as Peter initially refuses the grace of having Jesus wash his feet, and just as Martha initially cannot see "the better part," so we, too, can refuse Jesus' attempt to gently challenge us into letting go of our preoccupations and recognizing what we are missing. Weary, beleaguered, overwhelmed, we, too, can miss— or even unwittingly refuse—the gift of grace. We can refuse to be ministered to, even when accepting ministration will help us become better servants.

How can we avoid this trap? We can be more like Mary. Put aside time for the Lord. Sit at His feet. Read His words. Contemplate His teachings. Live in the present and absorb His presence. Let go the worries and preoccupations of our world for an hour or two and embrace the things of God's world. In that way, we fill ourselves with the grace needed to bring the two worlds together in love and service.

Grace and Provision

> Therefore, do not worry, saying, "What will we eat?" or "What will we drink?" or "What will we wear?" For it is the Gentiles who strive for all these things; and indeed your heavenly Father knows that you need all these things. But strive first for the kingdom of God and his righteousness, and all these things will be given to you as well. (Mt 6:31–33)

It is not easy to stop worrying about our physical needs. It is harder to ignore the siren call of money, status, and possessions. It is harder still to let go of anxiety and worry about those whom we care for, and who depend on us. After all, our own religion tells us to be responsible for ourselves and others. And therein lies a cruel problem. Most of us are not truly greedy, but we've been taught the value of independence; many of us believe that money, to a real extent, is freedom—or even worse, that money is the measure of the love we have for those who depend on us.

God understands our human nature. He understands our fears and our desires. He understands when our fears and desires merge. However, the Lord asks us to put them into perspective, to realize that everything we have is from Him and that He makes provision for us. First, Jesus tells us, we are to seek the kingdom of God, to serve God, and God will take care of our needs.

Is it even possible to believe this in our day and age? Does anyone have that kind of faith? It is a faith that requires a depth of grace many of us can only imagine. To live in utter dependence on God is to live in the highest level of grace; and yet, in reality, we all live in utter dependence on God. It is just that only a few of us realize this and acknowledge it in the way we live. The rest of us struggle to maintain our sense of human control, our false sense of autonomy. But we cannot be, or have being, independent of God and really, why would we want to?

My good friend Lynn Holm lives in complete dependence on God and has done so for many decades since he decided as a youngster to claim God as his one, true Father. He believes that God will provide not only for him and his family, but also for his works of service to the Lord. He never worries about where his money will come from or whether he will have enough to support those he serves. He moves forward generously and without hesitation, confident that God; will supply whatever he needs.

And it works! Time and again, God accommodates Lynn and his work. Sometimes, bags of groceries appeared on his porch while he and his wife were ministering to a community that couldn't afford to pay them enough. While Lynn and his family were on missions in Uganda, the Lord's spirit protected them by standing between the family and angry rebels. Cash was deposited into his bank account just when he needed a new appliance or to have his stove fixed. Clearly, God has cleared the way for Lynn to serve.

At times it can feel a bit difficult to be Lynn's friend, especially if you are occasionally sad and angry and skeptical like me. I'm a bit more like Lynn's late wife, who wanted to stay up all night and see who left the groceries on the porch! (He didn't let her.) I have a hard time trusting so fully, believing so utterly, giving up my own power so readily. Lynn's example gives me something to shoot for, while at the same time, I remind myself that God accepts me where I am and how I am . . . as long as I am at least trying.

Lynn is filled with grace. He believes that his home, his car, and everything he owns belong to God, and he depends upon God to make him a good steward of these earthly things. He doesn't question God's provisions. He doesn't doubt that they will be there when he needs them. In return, he is constantly giving. Witnessing his life helps me move a little more in the right direction with my life.

That stove, paid for with money that appeared in his bank account, produces food to cheer the spirits and nourish the bodies of hundreds on a regular basis. So I try to remember to put some food aside for the homeless-shelter residents. He gives away his time, his prayers, even his sleep, spending long hours communicating with God who sometimes wakes him just to pray for someone in need. So I try to spend a moment praying for someone who really annoys me during the day. It's not always easy to have a model like Lynn in one's life; but it can be just the challenge we all need.

Grace in Action

Grace is lived out in many forms. If Lynn Holm lives out a gentle and fearless grace, Jerry Lowney lives out a fierce and fearless grace, serving with unwavering determination. Doctor Jeremiah Lowney is not bashful about pointing out that he shares a name with one of the most prescient and irritating great prophets of old: Jeremiah. And like Jeremiah, Jerry doesn't quit, regardless of the obstacles he faces.

His commitment to service was actually born from an obstacle. A successful Connecticut orthodontist, husband, and father of four, he learned in 1981 that he had bladder cancer. He was given six months to live. The next year he fulfilled a commitment to spend a week in Haiti on a medical mission. He was barely finished with his treatment, hardly recovered from the surgery, and his family wondered if he could even care for himself—never mind perform dental procedures in the teeming alleys of Port-au-Prince. But Jerry's need to pay back for all the blessings of his life—from struggling to rise out of the slums of Fall River, Massachusetts, to beating cancer—drove him to make the Haiti mission. For a week, he and his son worked in the streets of Port-au-Prince; and when he returned to Connecticut, dirty and exhausted, he knew his life would never be the same.

He'd opened himself to grace, and it had bowled him over. For the past thirty years, Jerry and his family have been serving God in Haiti, moving from Port-au-Prince to the rural northwest region of Jérémie where he founded the Haitian Health Foundation (HHF). Working initially with sisters sent by Mother Teresa, Jerry has transformed what began as a week of dental work into a large, thriving clinic, food-distribution center, several schools, and a center for prenatal and postnatal care. That just begins to describe the aid he and the foundation have brought to nearly a quarter of a million impoverished Haitians. Armed only with grace, he has broken through barriers that the state and even the Church could not.

Like the best of all servants, he has brought others to his work, building a volunteer corps starting first with his family and extending to neighbors, colleagues, associates, and total strangers who hear about HHF and want to support its mission. Jerry and his family have taken countless volunteers to Haiti on quarterly trips that have changed the lives of the volunteers as often as they have saved the lives of Haitians. The grace that enfolds him draws others and allows them to take steps toward service that might otherwise have frightened them away.

It is worth noting that both Lynn Holm and Jerry Lowney committed themselves to God during a crisis in their respective lives. Few of us have the courage to live as these men do. Still, they demonstrate that it is possible, and that it is a choice to live gracefully. If these men had responded to the difficulties they faced with anger, bitterness, or resentment, their stories would have had quite different endings. How do we want our stories to end?

Saint Peter

Those of us who need to learn to accept grace couldn't have a better or more encouraging model than Saint Peter. How wonderful for us to know that the man Jesus selected to lead His church was the same man who put his foot in it again and again and again. Stubborn, impulsive Peter, determined to bluster his way through, always ready to add his two cents, is a shining beacon to us. In choosing the apostle who is arguably the most human in the gospels, Jesus gives us hope for the transformative power of grace in our own human natures.

Repeatedly, we see Jesus patiently teaching Peter. When Peter, feeling particularly magnanimous, suggests to Jesus that he is willing to forgive those who sin against him seven times, Jesus calmly blows this theory away, replying to Peter, "Not seven times, but, I tell you, seventy-seven times" (Mt 18:22). Peter is probably stunned; he can't believe that he hasn't gotten it right in his incredibly generous offer to forgive more than once. Does he understand Jesus' message that it is only through grace that he will be able to forgive once, seven times, or seventy-seven times? Do we?

Perhaps the most entertaining, and yet profound, image of Peter struggling with the grace the Lord offers occurs when Jesus comes to the apostles at night while they are at sea. When Peter sees Jesus walking on the water, he says,

> Lord, if it is you, command me to come to you on the water. He said, "Come." So Peter got out of the boat, started walking on the water, and came toward Jesus. But when he noticed the strong wind, he became frightened, and beginning to sink, he cried out, "Lord, save me!" Jesus immediately reached out his hand and caught him, saying to him, "You of little faith, why did you doubt?" (Mt 14:28–31)

Peter senses that Jesus' grace will sustain him, so he plunges out of the boat, but like many of us, once in the thick of things, his certainty deserts him. Jesus, again with great patience and probably heaving a sigh of resignation, scoops up this beloved apostle and asks why he doubted.

Is this the first pope, a doubter? Yes, and not only a doubter, but a denier. It is during the central crisis of Jesus and Peter's lives, that this apostle once again flees grace. But it will be the last time. Jesus, knowing the test His chosen apostle will undergo, gives Simon Peter a few words to hang onto during His Last Supper with the disciples:

> Simon, Simon, listen! Satan has demanded to sift all of you like wheat, but I have prayed for you that your own faith will not fail; and you, when once you have turned back, strengthen your brothers. And he said to him, "Lord, I am ready to go with you to prison and to death!" Jesus said, "I tell you, Peter, the cock will not crow this day, until you have denied three times that you know me." (Lk 22:31–34)

And so it happens. Peter not only denies Jesus three times, he denies Him dramatically and with an oath. His fear overcomes his ability to rely on grace. During the last denial, Jesus turns to look at Peter. It is this look that breaks Peter, and in his weakness and weeping, fear begins to be purged and room is made for grace.

Jesus is not done with Peter. Even while predicting Peter's denial, Jesus also gives him those words of assurance: that Peter's faith would hold. After His resurrection, Jesus seals this confirmation, taking Peter aside and making him repeat three times a declaration of love for Jesus. Even here, Peter is still Peter; we read that he is hurt and frustrated that the Lord is asking him thrice: "Simon son of John, do you love me?" (Jn 21:17). But Jesus, in using this formal language, is allowing Peter to renounce his three denials and assume the mantle of leadership. Peter will still need infusions of grace, a process that will be completed when the Holy Spirit descends upon him; but Jesus is making it clear that He has chosen this formerly graceless man to feed His sheep, tend His flock, and follow Him. From here on, Peter will never turn back.

Rewards of Grace

Grace will not always lead us onto easy roads. In fact, there will be more challenges than we can likely foresee. However, there will also be benefits that we cannot imagine. People who serve sometimes talk about how they are blessed through their service and by the people they serve. This can be as simple as people saying, "God bless you," when you give them a dollar or two, or serve them a meal; or it may be as intense as having your life changed by those you serve.

Jerry Lowney handily deflects any compliments paid to him about his work in Haiti by declaring that he is the one who is blessed by the Haitians and those who've joined him in serving them. He is not being modest—Jerry will be the first to say that he lacks the gene for modesty. He is simply being honest. From the moment he set up a makeshift dental chair in the streets of Port-au-Prince nearly thirty years ago, his life has been transformed by the people he's encountered: "They've helped me and they've blessed me and they've humbled me," he says, "and my family, thank God, has been extremely enriched by this experience. The foundation has become part of our family and the work is central to who we are."

Jerry is often asked why God allows people to experience poverty like that of the Haitians. He has a ready answer, but one he's thought about for some time. Jerry thinks it likely that the poor exist for us. They exist so that we can know the value of helping them. The poor exist, he thinks, because we need to be saved, and they are the vehicles through which we can work out and express our salvation.

This is a bold concept, and one with the potential to arouse strong opinions both in support and in opposition. But what if it is true? What if when Jesus tells the apostles, "For you always have the poor with you, and you can show kindness to them whenever you wish" (Mk 14:7), He was not merely reprimanding them for grumbling about the cost of perfume? Could it be that Jesus was showing them their future, showing us our future? We do, indeed, still have the poor with us, in untold numbers. Are they the gift through which we draw closer to God? Are they a means of the very grace we need to serve them?

I help run a book club for seven or eight months a year at our homeless shelter in New London, and I know what Jerry Lowney and Lynn Holm mean about the surprising rewards of service. In fact, I no longer consider it service to sit with this group and talk about books or just about anything else. We are not your typical book club. We don't gather around an elegant dining-room table sipping wine: some of us have problems with alcohol, and well, we don't have an elegant dining-room table.

In the summer, while we slap mosquitoes, we drag our folding chairs out to the pastor's driveway, between a chain-link fence and vines of wild roses that inevitably stick one or two of us. In the winter, we meet in a stuffy hallway because the rest of the space is taken up with bunks and cots. We are not particularly attractive. It would be fair to describe us as a motley crew, usually dressed in sweat clothes or jeans. A couple of us manage to show up in work-casual dress, but the rest of us are just as likely to be wearing clothes someone gave us or that we bought at the Salvation Army store on Bank Street.

When outdoors, we conduct our meetings by the yellow light of one lonely overhead security lamp, and because most of us can't afford glasses, we squint and hold out our books or poetry at arm's length. Some of us live in the shelter, some in subsidized housing, and some have our own places. We don't just talk about books—although we do have a great deal of empathy for Eugene O'Neill's plays about his desperate, ruined family; and we are curious about Thomas Aquinas, who seems to be a kinder-than-usual sort of saint. We rant and rave . . . actually, I'm the one usually ranting and raving; the group is occasionally entertained by my antics and, so, they put up with me. We laugh at lot, frequently about things that others might find sad or dark or tragic. Some of us don't have much besides laughter, so we like to use it when we can.

We pray together and laugh then, too, because we know God is in on all good jokes. We learn a great deal from each other, and I am probably the one who learns the most. One night last summer, I learned how profound a gift grace can be. It had grown dark and the thickly leafed trees surrounding us allowed only a glimpse of a full moon. We were sitting in a circle, and there was a rare moment of silence. In that instant, time stood still for me, and I believe God allowed me to see the men and women in my group the way He sees them. I looked around at each of them, and suddenly, they seemed inexpressibly beautiful to me, as though they were a gathering of saints painted by one of the great masters. The shadows carved in their cheekbones and foreheads, the sorrowful wisdom in their eyes, the expressions on their faces—all filled me with an extraordinary depth of love that took my breath away.

I have never told my book club about that experience, but that exquisite moment of grace is seared in my memory. I can still feel what I felt that night. Perhaps I should tell them, or maybe they will read this and know that the gift that God gave me through them that night was greater than anything I've given them. The grace to serve, when acted on, grows and re-dounds back upon the one who serves until a constantly ex-panding circle of grace and service sustains and allows us to live the rule of love which Jesus laid down.

Psalm 37:1–9, 18–19, 23–26, 39–40

Do not fret because of the wicked;
do not be envious of wrongdoers,
for they will soon fade like the grass,
and wither like the green herb.
Trust in the Lord, and do good;
so you will live in the land,
and enjoy security.
Take delight in the Lord,
and he will give you the desires of your heart.
Commit your way to the Lord;
trust in him, and he will act.
He will make your vindication shine like the light,
and the justice of your cause like the noonday.
Be still before the Lord, and wait patiently for him;
do not fret over those who prosper in their way,
over those who carry out evil devices.
Refrain from anger, and forsake wrath.
Do not fret—it leads only to evil.
For the wicked shall be cut off,
but those who wait for the Lord
shall inherit the land. . . .
The Lord knows the days of the blameless,
and their heritage will abide forever;
they are not put to shame in evil times,

in the days of famine they have abundance. . . .
Our steps are made firm by the Lord,
when he delights in our way;
though we stumble, we shall not fall headlong,
for the Lord holds us by the hand.
I have been young, and now am old,
yet I have not seen the righteous forsaken
or their children begging bread.
They are ever giving liberally and lending,
and their children become a blessing. . . .
The salvation of the righteous is from the Lord;
he is their refuge in the time of trouble.
The Lord helps them and rescues them;
he rescues them from the wicked, and saves them,
because they take refuge in him.

Service Prayer

God, giver of grace, prepare me to receive Your gift. Help me to understand that all good things come from You, starting with grace. Let me recognize the opportunities You provide for me. Help me to realize that grace is available to me if only I seek and accept it. When I have opened myself to Your saving grace, let me shine forth so that others may become aware of Your gift and seek it for themselves. Let everyone who meets me know that I am Yours by the gracefulness through which I live my life.

Questions

- What does grace mean to you? When you act in the spirit of God's grace, how do you feel?
- Are you a Martha or a Mary? Do you resist opportunities to receive grace because you are too busy? Is that a way of running away from God's gift?

Service Suggestions

- Prepare yourself to receive the gift of grace that will strengthen you for service. Set aside grace-time for you to open yourself to God and seek God's presence. Depending upon your habits and lifestyle, this grace-time might involve quiet prayer, meditation, a walk or bike ride, time in a church or another sacred place. Use the time consciously to ask God for this gift and open yourself to receiving it. Trust God to answer your prayer and provide for your needs.

- Allow someone else to treat you gracefully. Jesus washed the feet of the apostles, but it's unlikely you'll find someone willing to do that for you—except on Holy Thursday. In the meantime, recognize and embrace grace when it comes to you through someone else: an unexpected smile, someone helping you with groceries, a moving sermon, a material gift given with great love, an unsolicited kindness from a family member, friend, or even a stranger.

Move Forward

What good is it, my brothers and sisters, if you say you have faith but do not have works? Can faith save you? If a brother or sister is naked and lacks daily food, and one of you says to them, "Go in peace; keep warm and eat your fill," and yet you do not supply their bodily needs, what is the good of that? So faith by itself, if it has no works, is dead.

JAMES 2:14–17

Some biblical scholars believe that the James who wrote this passage was a cousin, or as he is referred to in scripture, a brother of Jesus. It is easy to believe that the author was close to Jesus because he is making a plea for Jesus' central concern: helping others. While Saint Paul waxes lyrical, intellectual, spiritual, scriptural, and historical in his many writings, James leaves us this one single letter. He cannot compete with Paul's brilliance or Peter's title or John's reputation as the one the Lord loves, but he can hammer home the message of his brother, Jesus: the correct expression of faith is service.

Reading the letter of James, we can almost sense his frustration. There was so much confusion in the early Church, as
is always the case when people try to adapt something sub-
lime—in this case, Jesus' life, teachings, suffering, death, and
resurrection—into something that will fit into, and make sense
in, the world. There were conflicts about whether Gentiles
could be admitted to the new Church, whether men had to
be circumcised, whether there should be geographical boundaries, whether Paul should submit to Peter, or whether Peter
should submit to Paul. This list went on and on as Paul traveled
all over the Mediterranean world, sometimes saying and doing and writing things that were countered by the first Jewish
Christians.

Writing in the midst of all of these divisions and controver-
sies, James is intently focused on one main thing: keeping the
new Church honest. To remain honest, members of the Church
must stay centered on Jesus' teaching about loving one another
and serving others. It almost seems as though James is tired of
all the wrangling among the apostles and various churches in
cities from Jerusalem to Rome. He seems dismayed that some
have taken Paul's assertion that salvation is by faith, not works,
and twisted it into a claim that serving others is not necessary.

James wants it be crystal clear: serving is necessary; in fact,
it is something that Jesus never stops teaching. James also may
be tired of all the competition between the early Christians.
With Paul in the picture, there is constant friction about which
apostle should be considered the most powerful, the closest to
God, the most successful. James is not interested in competition. He is interested on doing what Jesus tells us to do. James
wants to move forward in service, and to see the early Church
move with him.

We, too, can get caught up in rivalries. Who is the better
Christian? Who is the strongest servant? Who is most focused
on doing God's work? Who is donating the most time and treasure? Who is most successful on the road to service? As James
proves, all these questions are a waste of time. They don't move

us forward. In fact, they can dishearten and slow us down. Everyone who seeks to serve God must begin where he or she currently stands, and everyone who begins to serve, follows Jesus.

I sometimes find myself falling into the trap of comparing my service to that of others, and I am invariably disappointed and discouraged by the results. Am I as kind, generous, and utterly faithful as my friend Lynn Holm? Nope. Am I ready to hop on a plane and spend two weeks in Kenya helping to run Christian eye clinics like my friend Betty Pacelle? No way. Could I spend a week in a place like Haiti and transform the experience into a foundation like Jerry Lowney has with the Haitian Health Foundation? Doubt it. But none of these comparisons do me any good. Instead of helping me move forward, they are more likely to make me sit down and squander more time contemplating my limits.

When the apostles foolishly argue about who among them should be considered closest to Jesus, Jesus settles their argument brilliantly, telling them,

> "whoever wishes to become great among you must be your servant, and whoever wishes to be first among you must be slave of all. For the Son of Man came not to be served but to serve, and to give his life a ransom for many." (Mk 10:43–45)

In other words, quit wasting time on ridiculous speculation and rivalry, and start doing the work you have set out to do.

Reminders

> On the third day there was a wedding in Cana of Galilee, and the mother of Jesus was there. Jesus and His disciples had also been invited to the wedding. When the wine gave out, the mother of Jesus said to him, "They have no wine." And Jesus said to her, "Woman, what concern is that to you and to me? My hour has not yet come." His

mother said to the servants, "Do whatever he tells you." (Jn 2:1–5)

Even Jesus had to listen to the rare reminder to help others! God sends us reminders all the time, if we are willing to recognize them. The man with the sign at the intersection asking for work or money may annoy us a hundred times before we realize, at the hundred-and-first passing, that we are supposed to be the ones doing something to help him. We can repeatedly overlook the container for donated food at our grocery store before it dawns on us that we could easily buy a few extra items and throw them in. We may routinely ignore the special collection for the regional Catholic high school until it occurs to us that our wonderful babysitter goes to that school. We never even consider entering our city's annual walkathon to end cancer until our doctor sends us for a biopsy.

Every day, many times a day, God provides us with reminders that we are called to be servants. It may be easier to ignore the reminders, and we often do. But when the light does dawn on us, it can be a revelation. Perhaps it will be a small revelation, like feeling hungry and discovering that the cafe where you've stopped doesn't take credit cards and you have no cash . . . and millions of people are hungry or starving every day. Or, it may be a wrenching revelation, like when a young person you know attempts suicide and you are forced to acknowledge that you'd noticed he was upset, but hadn't had time to ask him about it.

These reminders are not always easy to accept and sometimes even unwelcome. But they are instructive and even necessary to keep us motivated to continue our service walk. Reminders are opportunities to receive and act upon grace; we should not be tempted to waste time and energy feeling guilty about what we haven't yet done. We are meant to be energized and not paralyzed by such reminders; they are signposts on the road to increased service.

Is Enough Ever Enough?

Can we ever give too much of ourselves to service? Not according to Jesus; He sets no boundaries on what a good servant should be willing to give. In fact, Jesus binds faith to service, a connection James will later reflect on in his letter. Luke tells us that when the apostles ask Jesus to increase their faith, He reminds them that their duties—like those of a slave—will be never-ending:

> "Do you thank the slave for doing what was commanded? So you also, when you have done all that you were ordered to do, say, 'We are worthless slaves; we have done only what we ought to have done!'"(Lk 17:9–10)

Stern as Jesus may sound in giving this reminder of what our work entails, He makes it clear that we must be vigilant in the pursuit and implementation of service. However, the Lord knows that we are human and thus capable of burning ourselves out and losing interest in the long haul of a life of ministry. With the grace to continue our work, He also gives us strategies and support in ways we may have yet to discover.

There have been times, especially recently, when Charlie and I have felt like giving up on service. The more involved we become in the bureaucracies built up around those who need help—from the court and corrections system to state and non-profit agencies—the more discouraged and weary we get. What can we do, after all, we ask ourselves, if the very systems set up to deal with issues like addiction, mental illness, poverty, and homelessness are moribund and dysfunctional? How much time are we supposed to give when it feels like we are beating our heads against a wall?

Recently, after Charlie spent countless hours and days trying to get a mentally ill friend out of jail and into a vibrant, proven mental-health program, the state corrections department fumbled the paperwork. Charlie came home and asked,

"Why are we doing this? It's not doing any good. Why aren't we having fun and taking care of our own needs?" Looking at him, I wondered the same thing. He looked haggard, angry, and most of all, depressed. I knew his words hadn't come from selfishness. We were both hurt and tired. Just a few days earlier we had visited our friend in prison and rejoiced with him about being released into this great program. Now, he was sitting in jail on the day he'd been told he would be on a bus to a new life filled with hope. We'd encouraged him in that belief, and we couldn't help but feel we'd let him down. We couldn't bear to think about the depth of his disappointment, or even what to do now.

It would be wonderful to report that the phone rang at that moment and the commissioner of the Corrections Department apologized for the error and told us our friend was on his way to the program. But that didn't happen. Such things rarely do. Instead, Charlie, who is an innately optimistic person, encountered a few people over the next couple of days who unwittingly reminded him of how successfully God had worked through him more than once to improve a handful of lives. He began to feel stronger, more cheerful. I, who am not an innately optimistic person, lay down to pray and asked God to give me something to hold onto. The words came into my mind: "Be kind." Not exactly the key to the mystery of life, I thought at first, but on reflection, I realized it just might be. In the face of the sorrow, poverty, rage, frustration, and despair that darkens so much of our world, it is the only Christian response.

And so, we've started the process of getting our friend back on the list for the mental-health program. It may take a while (it may not happen at all), but we're trying. We're back at the starting line, but we know what we have to do. Yesterday, in the middle of a lively discussion about the next step for our friend, I asked Charlie, "Remember when you were so upset and asked, 'Why aren't we having fun and taking care of our own needs?'" He looked at me and laughed wryly. "I know," he answered for us both, "for us, this is fun."

Rest Awhile

Jesus is the embodiment of service, and of the suffering servant, even to and through the point of death. Not even the cross or the tomb could keep Him from moving forward in service. Yet even Jesus, in the humanity He assumed, took time out to rest. Rest is vital to the process of service. Only God need never rest. Periodically, we will need to take time out and be still, to regroup, to calm our spirits, to purge ourselves of anger and frustration. The further we progress on the path of service, the deeper our commitment, the more challenges and obstacles we will confront. Increasingly, we will find ourselves unable to rely on our human nature. It is then we will become dependent on grace and rest.

Jesus knows this. Not only does He take time away from His work to rest and pray—sometimes taking aside His apostles and disciples for the same purpose—but also He cries out to all of us who follow Him: "Come to me, all you that are weary and are carrying heavy burdens, and I will give you rest. Take my yoke upon you, and learn from me; for I am gentle and humble in heart, and you will find rest for your souls" (Mt 11:28–29).

As servants, we can find rest in the Lord, but we must take the time to do so. If we don't rely on God's grace and rest, it is likely that we will be overwhelmed by the needs and pain of the world around us. Without rest, we are at risk of feeling bitter and disappointed when our efforts don't produce perfect results; or, for that matter, any results. Prayerful rest and time away will aid us in developing new perspectives and new coping skills. Taking time to rest is not a retreat, or a failure, or a repudiation of a service commitment; it is simply a way to embrace God's gift of grace in another form.

Saint Joseph and Mother Teresa

If we are looking for a model of moving forward in service to God, we need look no further than one of the most beloved—and, perhaps, taken-for-granted—saints. Saint Joseph is called many things: husband of Mary, foster father of Jesus, carpenter, traveler, worker; but most of all, Saint Joseph is the man who listens to God and does what God asks of him.

In the case of Joseph, God asked a lot. Regardless of how difficult the challenges, how long the commitment, and how seemingly small the reward (in the eyes of the world), Joseph first lifts his head up to hear God and then puts his head down, moving forward to do God's work.

How hard it must have been! How conflicted Joseph must have felt when God sent an angel in a dream to assert that his pregnant fiancée was carrying the Son of God and had not been unfaithful! After all, Joseph was only human. Even after he struggled with his own doubts, he had to know that their entire community would believe that he had been cuckolded and that he was marrying a "tainted" woman. Yet after waking from the dream, without a thought for his own reputation or the mockery he would face, Joseph did not hesitate or attempt to deny God's wishes. Instead, "he did as the angel of the Lord commanded him; he took her as his wife, but had no marital relations with her until she had borne a son; and he named him Jesus" (Mt 1:24–25).

Next, God will ask something even greater of Joseph. Soon after the infant Jesus was born, an angel of the Lord again comes to Joseph in a dream. This time it is not just Joseph's pride that is on the line, but his livelihood, his heritage, his entire way of life. King Herod is looking for Jesus in order to kill Him, the angel tells Joseph, and the only way to escape Herod is to move to a different country—not a different town, not even a different region, but a different country—Egypt. Egypt is the place where God had to all but destroy Pharaoh and his government in order to free the Jewish people from slavery. It is the place that Jews must have detested and despised and feared.

Imagine the questions that must have come into Joseph's human mind. What would happen to them in Egypt, of all places? How would he protect Mary and her Son in that foreign

land where false deities abound? Would he find work as a carpenter? As it was, his was not a high-earning or prestigious
trade, but at least among his own people he would have work.
Would the Egyptians even hire him? If not, how would he earn
bread for his precious family? And of course, how could he say
goodbye to all he had known: his family, his work, his community, and his place of worship?

Yet, upon waking, Joseph did not wait even for dawn: "Then
Joseph got up, took the child and his mother by night, and
went to Egypt, and remained there until the death of Herod"
(Mt 2:14–15). There would be more angelic dreams that would
burden Joseph's life. After Herod's death, Joseph is told to up-
root his small family again, leave behind what success and
routine he had developed in Egypt, and return to Israel. But
even then, Joseph is not allowed to resume the life he had left
behind, for in another dream, he is warned not to go to Judea
because Jesus would still be in danger there. So Joseph goes to
Galilee to begin again in Nazareth, one of the most inhospi-
table and arid regions of Israel.

We never hear of a word of complaint or doubt from Joseph, no matter what he might have felt. Joseph remains stoic
in his difficult service when a few years later, as Luke tells us,
Jesus quietly stays behind at the temple in Jerusalem after His
parents have begun the long journey home. Joseph and Mary
return in a panic to find their young son teaching the elders
in the temple. Mary chastises Jesus for worrying them. Jesus
replies coolly, "Why were you searching for me? Did you not
know that I must be in my Father's house?"(Lk 2:49). We read
of no reaction from Joseph: no anger, no hurt, no reproach.

This isn't to say that Joseph never felt uncertainty, hurt, anger, or dismay at the many unexpected turns his life had taken.
In all likelihood, he felt all this and more, and still Joseph continued to do God's will—and by everything we know—with
good humor and cheer. How? Clearly, Joseph trusted God with
a depth of trust that many of us may find hard to achieve. But
with the same grace that Joseph accepted from God, we can

seek that depth. It is no mistake that one of Joseph's titles is Saint Joseph the Worker. The feast day is celebrated on May 1. He is also the patron saint of a happy death. Those who manage to serve God as Joseph did will be granted the grace to live peacefully and die happily, in the knowledge that they have done the work the Lord has asked of them.

Not all who dedicate their lives to serving God will spend every moment in peaceful bliss, and it is good for those of us who have not achieved Joseph's single-mindedness to remember this. One of the finest recent examples of a saintly servant who suffered for, and in, her ministry is Mother Teresa. Even as she spent most of her life serving God's poorest, sickest, most rejected people, she suffered her own spiritual pain. After her death, we read of a diary in which she expresses feeling separated from God even as she does His work, work that few would have taken on.

While some have used the revelation of Mother Teresa's pain to disparage faith, I think it is quite the opposite. Many saints and servants suffer dark nights of the soul, when they feel confused or separated from God. Such feelings can be a mark of God, borne by those who struggle in God's service especially in following the commandment of Jesus, who suffered beyond human endurance in service. Saints and servants like Mother Teresa, who continue to minister despite their pain and feelings of distance from God, are a priceless example for those of us who also experience this admittedly frightening storm.

Encourage One Another

The difficulties of ministering to others, the agonies of doubt, and the challenges of the world are all reasons we must encourage one another to continue moving forward in service. On the occasions when I have wrestled with my own dark nights of the soul, I always return to one certainty about what God wants of us. We know with absolute confidence that God calls us to serve one another, strangers, and those in need.

Theologians and biblical commentators can argue about interpretations, theories, and who wrote what passages in the New Testament, but Jesus' message about how we are to act could not be clearer.

There is a good reason Jesus chose apostles and disciples and sent them out together. He knew that if His followers were to move forward in serving Him and living out His teachings, they would need to help and support one another. They would need to talk and walk and eat with each other. They would have to pray together and urge one another to pray. They would have to carry the slack for those who needed to rest or regroup. They would need to reflect the Spirit to one another so as to ignite and enliven the faith of their sisters and brothers.

We, today, are Jesus' disciples. We are called to light the flame of service for one another and then to minister together to those in need. As He did with the disciples, Jesus gathers us together in many ways: as coworkers in soup kitchens and homeless shelters; as volunteers and mentors and tutors; as contributors of time and money; as administrators and board members; as deacons and council members; as listeners and pray-ers; as spreaders of the Good News. If every person who reads this book takes a step on the road to service, and encourages another to do so, we will make blessed progress on living the Word of God as Jesus gave it to us. We are all unfinished servants, and as long as we continue to put ourselves in God's hands, by His gift of grace, we bring earth that much closer to heaven.

Psalm 119:1–8, 25–38, 65–68, 71–77

Happy are those whose way is blameless,
who walk in the law of the Lord.
Happy are those who keep his decrees,
who seek him with their whole heart,
who also do no wrong,
but walk in his ways.

You have commanded your precepts
to be kept diligently.
O that my ways may be steadfast
in keeping your statutes!
Then I shall not be put to shame,
having my eyes fixed on all your commandments.
I will praise you with an upright heart,
when I learn your righteous ordinances.
I will observe your statutes;
do not utterly forsake me. . . .

My soul clings to the dust;
revive me according to your word.
When I told of my ways, you answered me;
teach me your statutes.
Make me understand the way of your precepts,
and I will meditate on your wondrous works.
My soul melts away for sorrow;
strengthen me according to your word.
Put false ways far from me;
and graciously teach me your law.
I have chosen the way of faithfulness;
I set your ordinances before me.
I cling to your decrees, O Lord;
let me not be put to shame.
I run the way of your commandments,
for you enlarge my understanding.

Teach me, O Lord, the way of your statutes,
and I will observe it to the end.
Give me understanding, that I may keep your law
and observe it with my whole heart.
Lead me in the path of your commandments,
for I delight in it.
Turn my heart to your decrees,

and not to selfish gain.
Turn my eyes from looking at vanities;
give me life in your ways.
Confirm to your servant your promise,
which is for those who fear you. . . .

You have dealt well with your servant,
O Lord, according to your word.
Teach me good judgment and knowledge,
for I believe in your commandments.
Before I was humbled I went astray,
but now I keep your word.
You are good and do good; teach me your statutes. . . .
It is good for me that I was humbled,
so that I might learn your statutes.
The law of your mouth is better to me
than thousands of gold and silver pieces.
Your hands have made and fashioned me;
give me understanding that I may learn your commandments.
Those who fear you shall see me and rejoice,
because I have hoped in your word.
I know, O Lord, that your judgments are right,
and that in faithfulness you have humbled me.
Let your steadfast love become my comfort
according to your promise to your servant.
Let your mercy come to me, that I may live;
for your law is my delight.

Service Prayer

Jesus, it is sometimes difficult to follow You, and yet I want to continue on the path You've shown me. Give me the strength, Lord. When I grow tired or discouraged, give me new energy. When I am angry or frustrated, surround me with grace and peace. When I need to rest, provide me with the place and time.

When I am frightened or worried for myself, ease my fears and lend me Your courage. When I stumble and falter, lift me up and straighten my stride. Most of all, Lord, keep me near to You and let me make the choice every day to take Your hand.

Questions

- When you are frustrated or tired of a situation that does not involve service, how do you deal with it? Could you adapt some of those coping mechanisms to apply to service-related obstacles?

- Have you felt joy, a sense of accomplishment, and/or a deepening of your faith through your service? If so, can you use these feelings as inspiration to move forward in your service journey?

Service Suggestions

- Take three sheets of paper. On each sheet write one way in which you serve—or wish to serve. Next, on each page list obstacles that may hinder your serving in that way. Then, on each page, list strategies for overcoming each obstacle should it materialize. For example, one strategy might be to ask others in that area of service for help or advice; if so, make a list of such people and ways to contact them. Or maybe you will need to take time apart to rest and seek God's grace for a renewed commitment. Note how and where you will do that. Finally, on each sheet of paper, list the good feelings you've experienced, or hope to experience going forward from that act of service. Use these lists as resources when needed.

- Rejoice and give thanks that you are following Jesus' way and becoming a true disciple in service.

Afterword

A Willing Heart offers answers to one of life's most urgent questions: what can we do for others? This book is a valuable manual for anyone who hopes to enrich their own life and the lives of others through service. With memorable stories and thought-provoking questions, *A Willing Heart* guides us in discovering for ourselves, both in secular and spiritual terms, how we can make a difference today.

As Marci Alborghetti writes, service to God and others is an integral part of faith. In the Judeo-Christian tradition, we share a deeply-held belief that all human beings are deserving of respect and dignity and that during our short time here on earth, we must do all we can in service to God by serving humanity. The expression of our aspirations for service in the Jewish tradition is reflected in the Hebrew phrase *tikkun olam*, which is translated "to improve the world," or "to repair the world," or mostly boldly, "to complete the Creation which God began." This phrase reminds us that we have both the opportunity and the responsibility to improve ourselves and the wider world around us. Our lives are a blessing; and with this blessing comes an obligation: to serve others and live each day as well, and as fully, as we possibly can.

A Willing Heart also embraces the great tradition of service that has long been essential to the American experience. From the moment of its creation, America has been defined not by our borders, but by our values, and our purpose, as they are expressed in our Declaration of Independence, which proclaims that we are all created equal and are endowed with equal rights and opportunities. In serving others and encouraging one another to serve, as this good book does, we take critical steps towards realizing the "more perfect union" our Founders envisioned.

As Marci Alborghetti teaches us through her own inspiring journey, ordinary people can make an impact on our communities and our society in extraordinary ways. Despite the busy lives Americans lead and the economic challenges we face today, millions of people find time to volunteer regularly in communities through religious, social, athletic, or service organizations. Each year, more and more Americans dedicate their time and energy to community service, to enable others to live more fully, with greater hope and opportunity. I am inspired by America's great tradition of service and very grateful to Marci Alborghetti for producing this important book which I believe will inspire many more Americans to take up the call for meaningful service.

In *A Willing Heart*, Marci Alborghetti helps us see that through service to others, we come to know ourselves more deeply and to enrich the world more fully.

We face serious challenges today, but as this book reminds us, we also live in a time of great possibility. *A Willing Heart* leaves us with a timeless message: the best way to express our gratitude for all of the blessings of this life is not to profess our faith with words, but to act on that gratitude.

Senator Joseph I. Lieberman

Notes

1. Frank Rivers, T*he Way of the Owl: Succeeding with Integrity in a Conflicted World* (New York: HarperSanFrancisco, 1996).

2. Paul Tillich, *The Eternal Now* (London: Scm Press, 2002).

MARCI ALBORGHETTI has written hundreds of articles and essays on a wide range of matters covering religion, spirituality, social justice, diversity, and business. She has worked in public information and development and ran her own writing business for ten years. Over the past decade, Alborghetti has had fourteen books published including a biography, two short works of religious fiction, and a bestselling work of non-fiction titled *Prayer Power: How to Pray When You Think You Can't*. Her latest novel, *The Christmas Glass*, was released in 2009 by Guideposts/Ideals Publications, and she contributes regularly to *Daily Guideposts*. *Three Kings Day*, Alborghetti's sequel to *The Christmas Glass*, will be published in fall 2011.

Founded in 1865, Ave Maria Press,
a ministry of the Congregation of
Holy Cross, is a Catholic publishing
company that serves the spiritual and
formative needs of the Church and its
schools, institutions, and ministers;
Christian individuals and families; and
others seeking spiritual nourishment.

For a complete listing of titles from

Ave Maria Press

Sorin Books

Forest of Peace

Christian Classics

visit www.avemariapress.com

ave maria press® / Notre Dame, IN 46556
A Ministry of the Indiana Province of Holy Cross